THE LORD OF DYNEVOR

A Tale of the Times of Edward the First

EVELYN EVERETT-GREEN

1st WORLD
LIBRARY
Literary Society

The Lord of Dynevor

Evelyn Everett-Green

© 1st World Library, 2007
PO Box 2211
Fairfield, IA 52556
www.1stworldlibrary.com
First Edition

LCCN: 2007930782

Softcover ISBN: 978-1-4218-4820-4
Hardcover ISBN: 978-1-4218-4723-8
eBook ISBN: 978-1-4218-4917-1

Purchase *"The Lord of Dynevor"*
as a traditional bound book at:
www.1stWorldLibrary.com/purchase.asp?ISBN=978-1-4218-4820-4

1st World Library is a literary, educational organization
dedicated to:

- Creating a free internet library of downloadable ebooks

- Hosting writing competitions and offering book publishing
  scholarships.

Interested in more 1st World Library books? contact:
literacy@1stworldlibrary.com
Check us out at: www.1stworldlibrary.com

1st World Library Literary Society

Giving Back to the World

"If you want to work on the core problem, it's early school literacy."

- James Barksdale, former CEO of Netscape

"No skill is more crucial to the future of a child, or to a democratic and prosperous society, than literacy."

- Los Angeles Times

"Literacy... means far more than learning how to read and write... The aim is to transmit... knowledge and promote social participation."

- UNESCO

"Literacy is not a luxury, it is a right and a responsibility. If our world is to meet the challenges of the twenty-first century we must harness the energy and creativity of all our citizens."

- President Bill Clinton

"Parents should be encouraged to read to their children, and teachers should be equipped with all available techniques for teaching literacy, so the varying needs and capacities of individual kids can be taken into account."

- Hugh Mackay

CHAPTER I

DYNEVOR CASTLE

"La-ha-hoo! la-ha-hoo!"

Far down the widening valley, and up the wild, picturesque ravine, rang the strange but not unmusical call. It awoke the slumbering echoes of the still place, and a hundred voices seemed to take up the cry, and pass it on as from mouth to mouth. But the boy's quick ears were not to be deceived by the mocking voices of the spirits of solitude, and presently the call rang out again with greater clearness than before:

"La-ha-hoo!"

The boy stood with his head thrown back, his fair curls floating in the mountain breeze, his blue eyes, clear and bright and keen as those of a wild eaglet, fixed upon a craggy ridge on the opposite side of the gorge, whilst his left hand was placed upon the collar of a huge wolfhound who stood beside him, sniffing the wind and showing by every tremulous movement his longing to be off and away, were it not for the detaining hand of his young master.

The lad was very simply dressed in a tunic of soft, well-dressed leather, upon the breast of which was stamped some device which might have been the badge of his house. His active limbs were encased in the same strong, yielding material, and the only thing about him which seemed to indicate rank or birth was a belt with a richly-chased gold clasp and a poniard with a jewelled hilt.

Perhaps the noble bearing of the boy was his best proof of right to the noble name he bore. One of the last of the royal house of Dynevor, he looked every inch a prince, as he stood bare-headed in the sunlight amidst the everlasting hills of his well-loved home, too young to see the clouds which were settling so darkly and so surely upon the bright horizon of his life—his dreams still of glory and triumph, culminating in the complete emancipation of his well-loved country from the hated English yoke.

The dog strained and whined against the detaining clasp upon his neck, but the boy held him fast.

"Nay, Gelert, we are not going a-hunting," he said. "Hark! is not that the sound of a horn? Are they not even now returning? Over yon fell they come. Let me but hear their hail, and thou and I will be off to meet them. I would they heard the news first from my lips. My mother bid me warn them. I wot she fears what Llewelyn and Howel might say or do were they to find English guests in our hall and they all unwarned."

Once more the boy raised his voice in the wild call which had awakened the echoes before, and this time his practised ear distinguished amongst the multitudinous replies an answering shout from human lips. Releasing Gelert, who dashed forward with a bay of delight, the lad commenced springing from rock to rock up the narrowing gorge, until he reached a spot where the dwindling stream could be crossed by a bound; from which spot a wild path, more like a goat track than one intended for the foot of man, led upwards towards the higher portions of the wild fell.

The boy sped onwards with the fleetness and agility of a born mountaineer. The hound bounded at his side; and before either had traversed the path far, voices ahead of them became distinctly audible, and a little group might be seen approaching, laden with the spoils of the chase.

In the van of the little party were three lads, one of whom bore so striking a resemblance to the youth who now hastened to meet them, that the relationship could not be for a moment doubted. As a matter of fact the four were brothers; but they followed two distinct types—Wendot and Griffeth being fair and bright haired, whilst Llewelyn and Howel (who were twins) were dark as night, with black hair and brows, swarthy skins, and something of the wildness of aspect which often accompanies such traits.

Wendot, the eldest of the four, a well-grown youth of fifteen, who was walking slightly in advance of his brothers, greeted Griffeth's approach with a bright smile.

"Ha, lad, thou shouldst have been with us! We have had rare sport today. The good fellows behind can scarce carry the booty home. Thou must see the noble stag that my bolt brought down. We will have his head to adorn the hall—his antlers are worth looking at, I warrant thee. But what brings thee out so far from home? and why didst thou hail us as if we were wanted?"

"You are wanted," answered Griffeth, speaking so that all the brothers might hear his words. "The mother herself bid me go in search of you, and it is well you come home laden with meat, for we shall need to make merry tonight. There are guests come to the castle today. Wenwynwyn was stringing his harp even as I came away, to let them hear his skill in music. They are to be lodged for so long as they will stay; but the manner of their errand I know not."

"Guests!" echoed all three brothers in a breath, and very eagerly; "why, that is good hearing, for perchance we may now learn some news. Come these strangers from the north? Perchance we shall hear somewhat of our noble Prince Llewelyn, who is standing out so boldly for the rights of our nation. Say they not that the English tyrant is on our borders now, summoning him to pay the homage he repudiates with scorn? Oh, I would that this were a message summoning all true Welshmen to take up arms in his quarrel! Would not I fly to his standard, boy though I be! And would I not shed the last drop of my blood in the glorious cause of liberty!"

Llewelyn was the speaker, and his black eyes were glowing fiercely under their straight bushy brows. His face was the least boyish of any of the four, and his supple, sinewy frame had much of the strength of manhood in it. The free, open-air life that all these lads had lived, and the training they had received in all martial and hardy exercises, had given them strength and height beyond their years. It was no idle boast on the part of Llewelyn to speak of his readiness to fight. He would have marched against the foe with the stoutest of his father's men-at-arms, and doubtless have acquitted himself as well as any; for what the lads lacked in strength they made up in their marvellous quickness and agility.

The love of fighting seemed born in all these hardy sons of Wales, and something of warfare was known to them even now, from the never-ending struggles between themselves, and their resistance of the authority, real or assumed, of the Lords of the Marches. But petty forays and private feuds with hostile kinsmen was not the kind of fighting these brothers longed to see and share. They had their own ideas

Evelyn Everett-Green

and aspirations, and eager glances were turned upon Griffeth, lest he might be the bearer of some glorious piece of news that would mean open warfare with England.

But the boy's face was unresponsive and even a little downcast. He gave a quick glance into the fierce, glowing face of Llewelyn, and then his eyes turned upon Wendot.

"There is no news like that," he said slowly. "The guests who have come to Dynevor are English themselves."

"English!" echoed Llewelyn fiercely, and he turned away with a smothered word which sounded like an imprecation upon all the race of foreigners; whilst Howel asked with quick indignation:

"What right have English guests at Dynevor? Why were they received? Why did not our good fellows fall upon them with the sword or drive them back the way they came? Oh, if we had but been there—"

"Tush, brother!" said young Griffeth quickly; "is not our father lord of Dynevor? Dost think that thou canst usurp his authority? And when did ever bold Welshmen fall upon unarmed strangers to smite with the sword? Do we make war upon harmless travellers—women and children? Fie upon thee! it were a base thought. Let not our parents hear thee speak such words."

Howel looked a little discomfited by his younger brother's rebuke, though he read nothing but sympathy and mute approbation in Llewelyn's sullen face and gloomy eyes. He dropped a pace or so behind and joined his twin, whilst Wendot and Griffeth led the way in front.

"Who are these folks?" asked Wendot; "and whence come

they? And why have they thus presented themselves unarmed at Dynevor? Is it an errand of peace? And why speakest thou of women and children?"

"Why, brother, because the traveller has his little daughter with him, and her woman is in their train of servants. I know not what has brought them hither, but I gather they have lost their road, and lighted by chance on Dynevor. Methinks they are on a visit to the Abbey of Strata Florida; but at least they come as simple, unarmed strangers, and it is the boast of Wales that even unarmed foes may travel through the breadth and length of the land and meet no harm from its sons. For my part I would have it always so. I would not wage war on all alike. Doubtless there are those, even amongst the English, who are men of bravery and honour."

"I doubt it not," answered Wendot, with a gravity rather beyond his years. "If all our mother teaches us be true, we Welshmen have been worse enemies to one another than ever the English have been. I would not let Llewelyn or Howel hear me say so, and I would fain believe it not. But when we see how this fair land has been torn and rent by the struggles after land and power, and how our own kinsman, Meredith ap Res, is toying with Edward, and striving to take from us the lands we hold yet—so greatly diminished from the old portion claimed by the lords of Dynevor—we cannot call the English our only or even our greatest foes. Ah, if Wales would but throw aside all her petty feuds, and join as brothers fighting shoulder to shoulder for her independence, then might there be some hope! But now—"

Griffeth was looking with wide-open, wondering eyes into his brother's face. He loved and reverenced Wendot in a fashion that was remarkable, seeing that the elder brother was but two years and a half his senior. But Wendot had always been grave and thoughtful beyond his years, and had

Evelyn Everett-Green

been taken much into the counsels of his parents, so that questions which were almost new to the younger lad had been thought much of by the eldest, the heir of the house of Dynevor.

"Why, brother, thou talkest like a veritable monk for learning," he said. "I knew not thou hadst the gift of such eloquent speech. Methought it was the duty of every free-born son of Wales to hate the English tyrant."

"Ay, and so I do when I think of his monstrous claims," cried Wendot with flashing eyes. "Who is the King of England that he should lay claim to our lands, our homage, our submission? My blood boils in my veins when I think of things thus. And yet there are moments when it seems the lesser ill to yield such homage to one whom the world praises as statesman and soldier, than to see our land torn and distracted by petty feuds, and split up into a hundred hostile factions. But let us not talk further of this; it cuts me to the heart to think of it. Tell me more of these same travellers. How did our parents receive them? And how long purpose they to stay?"

"Nay, that I have not heard. I was away over yon fell with Gelert when I saw the company approach the castle, and ere I could find entrance the strangers had been received and welcomed. The father of the maiden is an English earl, Lord Montacute they call him. He is tall and soldier-like, with an air of command like unto our father's. The damsel is a fair-faced maiden, who scarce opens her lips; but she keeps close to our mother's side, and seems loath to leave her for a moment. I heard her father say that she had no mother of her own. Her name, they say, is Lady Gertrude."

"A damsel at Dynevor," said Wendot, with a smile; "methinks that will please the mother well."

"Come and see," cried Griffeth eagerly. "Let us hasten down to the castle together."

It was easy work for the brothers to traverse the rocky pathway. Dangerous as the descent looked to others, they were as surefooted as young chamois, and sprang from rock to rock with the utmost confidence. The long summer sunlight came streaming up the valley in level rays of shimmering gold, bathing the loftier crags in lambent fire, and filling the lower lands with layers of soft shadow flecked here and there with gold. A sudden turn in the narrow gorge, through which ran a brawling tributary of the wider Towy, brought the brothers full in sight of their ancestral home, and for a few seconds they paused breathless, gazing with an unspeakable and ardent love upon the fair scene before them.

The castle of Dynevor (or Dinas Vawr = Great Palace) stood in a commanding position upon a rocky plateau overlooking the river Towy. From its size and splendour—as splendour went in those days—it had long been a favourite residence with the princes of South Wales; and in a recent readjustment of disputed lands, consequent upon the perpetual petty strife that was ruining the land, Res Vychan, the present Lord of Dynevor, had made some considerable sacrifice in order to keep in his own hands the fair palace of his fathers.

The majestic pile stood out boldly from the mountain side, and was approached by a winding road from the valley. A mere glance showed how strong was the position it occupied, and how difficult such a place would be to capture. On two sides the rock fell away almost sheer from the castle walls, whilst on the other two a deep moat had been dug, which was fed by small mountain rivulets that never ran dry; and the entrance was commanded by a drawbridge, whose frowning portcullis was kept by a grim warder looking fully equal to the office allotted to him.

Lovely views were commanded from the narrow windows of the castle, and from the battlements and the terraced walk that ran along two sides of the building. And rough and rude as were the manners and customs of the period, and partially uncivilized as the country was in those far-off days, there was a strong vein of poetry lying latent in its sons and daughters, and an ardent love for the beautiful in nature and for the country they called their own, which went far to redeem their natures from mere savagery and brute ferocity.

This passionate love for their home was strong in all the brothers of the house of Dynevor, and was deepened and intensified by the sense of uncertainty now pervading the whole country with regard to foreign aggression and the ever-increasing claims upon Welsh lands by the English invaders. A sense as of coming doom hung over the fair landscape, and Wendot's eyes grew dreamy as he stood gazing on the familiar scene, and Griffeth had to touch his arm and hurry him down to the castle.

"Mother will be wanting us," he said. "What is the matter, Wendot? Methinks I see the tears in thine eyes."

"Nay, nay; tears are for women," answered Wendot with glowing cheeks, as he dashed his hand across his eyes. "It is for us men to fight for our rightful inheritance, that the women may not have to weep for their desolated homes."

Griffeth gave him a quick look, and then his eyes travelled lovingly over the wide, fair scene, to the purple shadows and curling mists of the valley, the dark mysterious woods in front, the clear, vivid sunlight on the mountain tops, and the serried battlements of the castle, now rising into larger proportions as the boys dropped down the hillside towards the postern door, which led out upon the wild fell. There was something of mute wistfulness in his own gaze as he did so.

"Brother," he said thoughtfully, "I think I know what those feelings are which bring tears to the eyes of men—tears of which they need feel no shame. Fear not to share with me all thy inmost thoughts. Have we not ever been brothers in all things?"

"Ay, truly have we; and I would keep nothing back, only I scarce know how to frame my lips to give utterance to the thoughts which come crowding into my brain. But see, we have no time for communing now. Go on up the path to the postern; it is too narrow for company."

Indeed, so narrow was the track, so steep the uncertain steps worn in the face of the rock, so deep the fall if one false step were made, that few save the brothers and wilder mountaineers ever sought admission by the postern door. But Wendot and Griffeth had no fears, and quickly scaled the steps and reached the entrance, passing through which they found themselves in a narrow vaulted passage, very dark, which led, with many twists and turns, and several ascending stairs, to the great hall of the castle, where the members of the household were accustomed for the most part to assemble.

A door deeply set in an embrasure gave access to this place, and the moment it was opened the sound of a harp became audible, and the brothers paused in the deep shadow to observe what was going on in the hall before they advanced further.

A scene that would be strange and picturesque to our eyes, but was in the main familiar to theirs, greeted them as they stood thus. The castle hall was a huge place, large enough to contain a muster of armed men. A great stone staircase wound upwards from it to a gallery above. There was little furniture to be seen, and that was of a rude kind, though not lacking in a certain massiveness and richness in the matter of carving, which gave something baronial to the air of the place. The walls were adorned with trophies of all sorts, some composed of arms, others of the spoil of fell and forest. The skins of many savage beasts lay upon the cold stone flooring of the place, imparting warmth and harmony by the rich tints of the furs. Light was admitted through a row of narrow windows both above and below; but the vast place would have been dim and dark at this hour had it not been that the huge double doors with their rude massive bolts stood wide open to the summer air, and the last beams of the westering sun came shining in, lying level and warm upon the group at the upper end of the hall, which had gathered around the white-haired, white-bearded bard, who, with head thrown backwards, and eyes alight with strange passions and feelings, was singing in a deep and musical voice to the sound of his instrument.

Old Wenwynwyn was a study in himself; his flowing hair, his fiery eyes, his picturesque garb and free, untrammelled gestures giving him a weird individuality of his own. But it was not upon him that the eyes of the brothers dwelt, nor even upon the soldier-like figure of their stalwart father leaning against the wall with folded arms, and eyes shining with the patriotic fervour of his race. The attention of the lads was enchained by another and more sumptuous figure— that of a fine-looking man, approaching to middle life, who was seated at a little distance from the minstrel, and was smiling with pleasure and appreciation at the wild sweetness of the stream of melody poured forth.

One glance at the dress of the stranger would have been enough to tell the brothers his nationality. His under tunic, which reached almost to the feet, was of the finest cloth, and was embroidered along the lower border with gold thread. The sur-tunic was also richly embroidered; and the heavy mantle clasped upon the shoulder with a rare jewel was of some rich texture almost unknown to the boys. The make and set of his garments, and the jewelled and plumed cap which he held upon his knee, alike proclaimed him to be English; yet as he gazed upon the noble face, and looked into the clear depths of the calm and fearless eyes, Wendot felt no hostility towards the representative of the hostile race, but rather a sort of reluctant admiration.

"In faith he looks born to command," he whispered to Griffeth. "If all were like unto him—"

But the lad did not complete the sentence, for he had suddenly caught sight of another figure, another face, and he stopped short in a sort of bewildered amaze.

In Dynevor Castle there had never been a girl child to share the honours with her brothers. No sister had played in its halls, or tyrannized over the lads or their parents. And now when Wendot's glance fell for the first time upon this little fairy-like creature, this lovely little golden-haired, blue-eyed maiden, he felt a new sensation enter his life, and gazed as wonderingly at the apparition as if the child had been a ghost.

And the soft shy eyes, with their fringe of dark lashes, were looking straight at him. As he gazed the child suddenly rose, and darted towards the brothers as if she had wings on her feet.

"Oh, you have come back!" she said, looking from one to the other, and for a moment seeming puzzled by the likeness; "and—why, there are two of you," and the child broke into the merriest and silveriest of laughs. "Oh, I am so glad! I do like boys so much, and I never have any to play with at home. I am so tired of this old man and his harp. Please let me go somewhere with you," and she thrust her soft little

　　　　Evelyn Everett-Green

hand confidingly into Wendot's, looking up saucily into his face as she added, "You are the biggest; I like you the best."

Wendot's face glowed; but on the whole he was flattered by the attention and the preference of the little maiden. He understood her soft English speech perfectly, for all the Dynevor brothers had been instructed in the English tongue by an English monk who had long lived at the castle. Res Vychan, the present Lord of Dynevor, foresaw, and had foreseen many years, the gradual usurpation of the English, and had considered that a knowledge of that tongue would in all probability be an advantage to those who were likely to be involved in the coming struggle. The boys all possessed the quick musical ear of their race, and found no difficulty in mastering the language; but neither Llewelyn nor Howel would ever speak a single word of the hated tongue if they could help it, though Wendot and Griffeth conversed often with the old monk right willingly.

So as Wendot looked down into the bright little upturned face, he was able to reply readily and smilingly:

"Where would you like to go, little lady, and what would you like me to show you?"

"Oh, everything—all out there," said the little girl, with a wave of her hand towards the front door. "I want to go and see the sun. I am tired of it in here."

Wendot led the child through the hall, and out upon the great terrace which overlooked the steep descent to the valley and away to the glowing west. Griffeth followed, glad that his elder brother had been preferred before himself by the little maiden, yet half fascinated by her nameless charm. Wendot lifted her up in his strong arms to see over the wide stone balustrade, and she made him set her down there and perch himself by her side; for she seemed loath to go back to the hall again, and the boys were as willing as she to remain out in the open air.

"It is pretty here," said the child graciously; "I think I should like to live here sometimes, if it was always summer. Tell me your name, big boy. I hope it is not very hard. Some people here have names I cannot speak right."

"They call me Res Wendot," answered the lad; "generally Wendot at home here. This is Griffeth, my youngest brother. Those are not hard names, are they?"

"No, not very. And how old are you, Wendot?"

"I am fifteen."

"Oh, how big you are!" said the little lady, opening her eyes wide; "I thought you must be much older than that. I am twelve, and you can lift me up in your arms. But then I always was so little—they all say so."

"Yet you travel about with your father," said Wendot.

"I never did before; but this time I begged, and he took me. Sometimes he says he shall have to put me in a nunnery, because he has nobody to take care of me when he has to travel about. But I don't think I should like that; I would rather stay here."

Wendot and Griffeth laughed; but the child was not at all disconcerted. She was remarkably self possessed for her years, even if she was small of stature and infantile in appearance.

"What is your name?" asked Wendot; and the little maid

Evelyn Everett-Green

answered, with becoming gravity and importance:

"I am called Lady Gertrude Cherleton; but you may call me Gertrude if you like, because you are kind and I like you. Are there any more of you? Have you any sisters?"

"No; only two brothers."

"More brothers! and what are their names?"

"Llewelyn and Howel."

"Llewelyn? Why, that is the name of the Prince of North Wales that the king is going to fight against and conquer. Do you think when he has done so that he will come here and conquer you, too?"

Wendot's cheek burned a sudden red; but he made no reply, for at that moment a head suddenly appeared round an angle of the wall, and a heavy grip was laid upon the shoulder of the child. A wild face and a pair of flashing black eyes were brought into close proximity with hers, and a smothered voice spoke in fierce, low accents.

CHAPTER II

THE BROTHERS

"What is that you dare to say?"

The voice was harsh, the words were spoken with a rough accent, unlike the gentler tones of Wendot and Griffeth. The child uttered a little cry and shrank back away from the grip of the strong hand, and might have been in some danger of losing her balance and of falling over the balustrade, had not Wendot thrown a protecting arm round her, whilst pushing back with the other hand that of the rude interloper.

"Llewelyn! for shame!" he said in his own tongue. "Art thou a man, and claimest the blood of princes, and yet canst stoop to frighten an inoffensive child?"

"She spoke of conquest—the conquest of our country," cried Llewelyn fiercely, in the hated English tongue, scowling darkly at the little girl as he spoke. "Thinkest thou that I will stand patiently by and hear such words? What right hath she or any one besides to speak of that tyrant and usurper in such tones?"

"He is not a tyrant, he is not a usurper!" cried the little Lady Gertrude, recovering herself quickly, and, whilst still holding

Evelyn Everett-Green

Wendot by the hand, turning fearlessly upon the dark-faced lad who had startled and terrified her at the first. "I know of whom you are speaking—it is of our great and noble King Edward. You do not know him—you cannot know how great and good he is. I will not hear you speak against him. I love him next best to my own father. He is kind and good to everybody. If you would all give your homage to him you would be happy and safe, and he would protect you, and—"

But Llewelyn's patience was exhausted; he would listen no more. With a fierce gesture of hatred that made the child shrink back again he turned upon her, and it seemed for a moment almost as though he would have struck her, despite Wendot's sturdy protecting arm, had not his own shoulder been suddenly grasped by an iron hand, and he himself confronted by the stern countenance of his father.

"What means this, boy?" asked Res Vychan severely. "Art thou daring to raise thine arm against a child, a lady, and thy father's guest? For shame! I blush for thee. Ask pardon instantly of the lady and of her father. I will have no such dealings in mine house. Thou shouldst be well assured of that."

The black-browed boy was crimson with rage and shame, but there was no yielding in the haughty face. He confronted his father with flashing eyes, and as he did so he met the keen, grave glance of the stranger's fixed upon him with a calm scrutiny which aroused his fiercest rage.

"I will not ask pardon," he shouted. "I will not degrade my tongue by uttering such words. I will not—"

The father's hand descended heavily upon his son's head, in a blow which would have stunned a lad less hardy and hard-headed. Res Vychan was not one to be defied with impunity by his own sons, and he had had hard encounters of will before now with Llewelyn.

"Choose, boy," he said with brief sternness. "Either do my will and obey me, or thou wilt remain a close prisoner till thou hast come to thy senses. My guests shall not be insulted by thy forward tongue. Barbarous and wild as the English love to call us, they shall find that Res Vychan is not ignorant of those laws which govern the world in which they live and move. Ask pardon of the lady, or to the dungeon thou goest."

Llewelyn glanced up into his father's face, and saw no yielding there. Howel was making vehement signs to him which he and he alone could interpret. His other brothers were eagerly gazing at him, and Griffeth even went so for as to murmur into his ear some words of entreaty.

It seemed as though the silence which followed Res Vychan's words would never be broken, but at last the culprit spoke, and spoke in a low, sullen tone.

"I meant no harm. I would not have hurt her."

"Ask her pardon then, boy, and tell her so."

"Nay, force him no more," said the little lady, who was regarding this curious scene with lively interest, and who began to feel sorry for the dark wild boy who had frightened her by his vehemence before; "I was to blame myself. I should not have spoken as I did.

"Father, tell them how my tongue is always running away with me. Hast not thou told me a hundred times that it would get me into trouble one of these days? It is right that he should love his country. Do not think ill of him for that."

"Ay, let the lad go now, good friend," quoth Lord Montacute. "No doubt this little witch of mine was at the bottom of the mischief. Her tongue, as she truly says, is a restless and mischievous possession. She has found a stanch protector at least, and will come to no harm amongst thy stalwart lads. I could envy thee such a double brace of boys. I would it had pleased Providence to send me a son."

"Nay, father, say not so," cried little Lady Gertrude coaxingly. "I would not have a brother for all the world. Thou wouldst love him so well, if thou hadst him, that thou wouldst have none to spare for thy maid. I have seen how it ever is. I love to have all thy heart for mine own."

The father smiled, but Res Vychan's face was still severe, and he had not loosed his clasp upon Llewelyn's arm.

"Say that thou art sorry ere I let thee go," he said, in low but very stern tones; and after a moment's hesitation, Llewelyn spoke in audible tones.

"I am sorry," he said slowly; "I am sorry."

And then as his father's clasp upon his arm relaxed he darted away like an arrow from the bow, and plunged with Howel through a dark and gloomy doorway which led up a winding turret stair to a narrow circular chamber, which the brothers shared together.

"Sorry, sorry, sorry!" he panted fiercely; "ay, that indeed I am. Sorry that I did not wring her neck as the fowler wrings the neck of the bird his shaft hath brought down; sorry I did not cast her headlong down the steep precipice, that there might be one less of the hated race contaminating the air of our pure Wales with their poisonous breath. Sorry! ay, that I am! I would my hand had done a deed which should have set proud Edward's forces in battle array against us. I would that this tampering with traitors were at an end, and that we warriors of South Wales might stand shoulder to shoulder, firmly banded against the foreign foe. I would plunge a dagger in the false heart of yon proud Englishman as he lies sleeping in his bed tonight, if by doing so I could set light to the smouldering flame of national hatred.

"What sayest thou? Can we do nought to bring upon us an open war, which is a thousand times better than this treacherous, hollow peace? Our father and mother are half won over to the cause of slavery. They—"

Llewelyn paused, choking back the fierce tide of passion which went far to unman him. He had not forgotten the humiliation placed upon him so recently, when his father had compelled him to sue for pardon to an English maiden. His heart was burning, his soul was stirred to its depths. He had to stop short lest his passion should carry him away.

Howel seemed to understand him without the medium of words. The links which bound the twin brothers together were very subtle and very strong. If Llewelyn were the more violent and headstrong, Howel was more than his equal in diplomacy. He shared every feeling of his brother's heart, but he was less outspoken and less rash.

"I know what thou wouldst do," he said thoughtfully: "thou wouldst force upon our father a step which shall make a rupture with the English inevitable. Thou wouldst do a thing which should bring upon us the wrath of the mighty Edward, and force both ourselves and our neighbours to take arms against him. Is not that so?"

"Ay, truly; and could such a thing be, gladly would I lay down my life in the cause of liberty and freedom."

Howel was pondering deeply.

"Perchance it might be done," he said.

Llewelyn eagerly raised his head.

"Thinkest thou so? How?"

"I know not yet, but we shall have time for thought. Knowest thou that the maid will remain here beneath our mother's charge for a while, whilst our father goes forward as far as the Abbey of Strata Florida with yon stranger, to guide him on his way? The maid will remain here until her father's return."

"How knowest thou that?"

"I had it from Wenwynwyn's lips. He heard the discussion in the hall, and it seems that this Lord Montacute would be glad to be free of the care of the child for a while. Our mother delights in the charge of a little maid, and thus it will be as I have said."

A strange fire gleamed in Llewelyn's eyes. The brothers looked at each other a good while in silence.

"And thou thinkest—" said Llewelyn at last.

Howel was some time in replying, and his answer was a little indeterminate, although sufficiently significant.

"Why, the maid will be left here; but when her father returns to claim her, perchance she will not be found. If that were so, thinkest thou not that nought but open war would lie before us?"

Llewelyn's eyes glowed. He said not a word, and the darkness gathered round the boys in the narrow chamber. They thought not of descending or of asking for food, even after their day's hunting in the hills. They were hardy, and seasoned to abstemious ways, and had no room for thoughts of such a kind. Silence was settling down upon the castle, and they had no intention of leaving their room again that night. Dark thoughts were their companions as they undressed and made ready for bed; and hardly were they settled there before the door opened, and the old bard Wenwynwyn entered.

This old man was almost like a father to these boys, and Llewelyn and Howel were particularly attached to him and he to them. He shared to the full their ardent love for their country and their untempered hatred of the English race. He saw, as they did, nothing but ill in the temporizing attitude now to be found amongst the smaller Welsh chieftains with regard to the claims made by the English monarch; and much of the fierce hostility to be found in the boys had been the result of the lessons instilled into their mind by the wild-eyed, passionate old bard, one of the last of a doomed race.

"Wenwynwyn, is it thou?"

"Ay, boys, it is I. You did well to abstain from sitting at meat with the stranger tonight. The meat went nigh to choke me that was swallowed in his presence."

"How long stays he, contaminating our pure air?"

"He himself is off by sunrise tomorrow, and Res Vychan goes with him. He leaves behind the little maid in the care of thy mother."

A strange smile crossed the face of the old man, invisible in

Evelyn Everett-Green

the darkness.

"Strange for the parent bird to leave the dove in the nest of the hawk—the eyry of the eagle."

"Ha!" quoth Llewelyn quickly, "that thought hath likewise come to thee, good Wenwynwyn."

The old man made no direct response, but went on speaking in low even tones.

"The maid has dwelt in the household of the great king. She has played with his children, been the companion of the young princesses. She is beloved of them and of the monarch and his wife. Let them but hear that she is lost in the fastness of Dynevor, and the royal Edward will march in person to her rescue. All the country will rise in arms to defend itself. The north will join with the south, and Wales will shake off the hated foreign yoke banded as one man against the foreign foe."

The boys listened spellbound. They had often talked together of some step which might kindle the conflagration, but had never yet seen the occasion. Hot-headed, rash, reckless as were the youths; wild, tameless, and fearless as was the ancient bard; they had still been unable to hit upon any device which might set a light to the train. Discontent and resentment were rife all over the country, but it was the fashion rather to temporize with the invader than to defy him. There was a strong party gathering in the country whose policy was that of paying homage to Edward and retaining their lands under his protection and countenance, as being more truly patriotic and farsighted than continuing the old struggle for supremacy among themselves. This was a policy utterly incomprehensible both to the boys and the old man, and stirred the blood of the lads to boiling pitch.

"What can we do?" asked Llewelyn hoarsely.

"I will tell you," whispered the old man, approaching close to the bed whereon the brothers lay wide-eyed and broad awake. "This very night I leave the castle by the postern door, and in the moonlight I make my way to the commot of Llanymddyvri, where dwells that bold patriot Maelgon ap Caradoc. To him I tell all, and he will risk everything in the cause. It will be very simply done. You boys must feign a while—must feign friendship for the maid thus left behind. Your brothers have won her heart already; you must not be behind them. The dove must have no fear of the young eaglets. She has a high courage of her own; she loves adventure and frolic; she will long to stretch her wings, and wander amid the mountain heights, under the stanch protection of her comrades of Dynevor.

"Then listen, boys. The day will come when the thing is to be done. In some of the wild fastnesses of the upper Towy will be lurking the bold bands of Maelgon ap Caradoc. Thither you must lead the unsuspicious maid, first by some device getting rid of your brothers, who might try to thwart the scheme. These bold fellows will carry off the maid to the safe keeping of Maelgon, and once let her be his prisoner, there is no fear of her escaping from his hands. Edward himself and all his forces at his back will scarce wrest away the prize, and the whole country will be united and in arms ere it suffer the tyrant to march through our fair vales."

Whilst within this upper turret chamber this plot was being concocted against the innocent child by two passionate, hot-headed boys and one of the ancient race of bards, the little maiden was herself sleeping soundly and peacefully within a small inner closet, close to the room where Gladys, the lady of the castle, reposed; and with the earliest streak of dawn, when the child opened her eyes upon the strange bare walls

Evelyn Everett-Green

of the Welsh stronghold, the first thing that met her eyes was the sweet and gentle face of the chatelaine bending tenderly over her.

Although the present lady of Dynevor was the sister of the bold and fierce Llewelyn, Prince of North Wales, who gave more trouble to the King of England than did anybody else, she was herself of a gentle and thoughtful disposition, more inclined to advocate peace than war, and more far-seeing, temperate, and well-informed than most persons of her time, and especially than the women, who for the most part had but very vague ideas as to what was going on in the country.

She had had many thoughts herself during the still hours of this summer night, and when she bent over the sleeping child and wakened her by a kiss, she felt a strange tenderness towards her, which seemed to be reciprocated by the little one, who suddenly flung her arms about her neck and kissed her passionately.

"Is my father gone?" she asked, recollection coming back.

"Not gone, but going soon," answered the Lady of Dynevor, smiling; "that is why I have come to waken thee early, little Gertrude, that thou mayest receive his farewell kiss and see him ride away. Thou wilt not be grieved to be left with us for a while, little one? Thou wilt not pine in his absence?"

"Not if I have you to take care of me," answered the child confidingly—"you and Wendot and Griffeth. I am weary of always travelling on rough roads. I will gladly stay here a while with you."

There was the bustle of preparation going on in the hall when the lady descended with the child hanging on to her hand. Gertrude broke away and ran to her father, who was sitting at the board, with Wendot standing beside him listening eagerly to his talk. The boy's handsome face was alight, and he seemed full of eager interest in what was being said. Lord Montacute frequently raised his head and gave the lad a look of keen scrutiny. Even whilst caressing his little daughter his interest seemed to be centred in Wendot, and when at parting the lad held his stirrup for him, and gently restrained little Gertrude, who was in danger of being trampled on by the pawing charger, Lord Montacute looked for a moment very intently at the pair, and then let his glance wander for a moment over the grand fortress of Dynevor and the beautiful valley it commanded.

Then he turned once more to Wendot with a kindly though penetrating smile.

"In the absence of your father, Wendot, you are the master and guardian of this castle, its occupants and its treasures. I render my little daughter into your safe keeping. Of your hands I shall ask her back when I return in a week's time."

Wendot flushed with pleasure and gratification. What boy does not like the thought of being looked upon as his father's substitute? He raised his head with a gesture of pride, and clasped the little soft hand of Gertrude more closely in his.

"I will take the trust, Lord Montacute," he said. "I will hold myself responsible for the safety of Lady Gertrude. At my hands demand her when you return. If she is not safe and well, take my life as the forfeit."

Lord Montacute smiled slightly at the manly words and bearing of the lad, but he did not like him the less for either. As for little Gertrude, she gazed up into the bold bright face of Wendot, and clasping his hand in hers, she said:

Evelyn Everett-Green

"Am I to belong to you now? I think I shall like that, you are so brave and so kind to me."

The father gave the pair another of his keen looks, and rode off in the bright morning sunshine, promising not to be very long away.

"I shan't fret, now that I have you and the Lady of Dynevor," said the child confidingly to Wendot. "I've often been left for a long time at the palace with the ladies Eleanor and Joanna, and with Alphonso and Britton, but I shall like this much better. There is no governess here, and we can do as we like. I want to know everything you do, and go everywhere with you."

Wendot promised to show the little lady everything she wanted, and led her in to breakfast, which was a very important meal in those days. All the four brothers were gathered at the board, and the child looked rather shyly at the dark-browed twins, whom she hardly knew one from the other, and whom she regarded with a certain amount of awe. But there was nothing hostile in the manner of any of the party. Llewelyn was silent, but when he did speak it was in very different tones from those of last night; and Howel was almost brilliant in his sallies, and evoked many a peal of laughter from the lighthearted little maiden. Partings with her father were of too common occurrence to cause her much distress, and she was too well used to strange places to feel lost in these new surroundings, and she had her own nurse and attendant left with her.

Full of natural curiosity, the child was eager to see everything of interest near her temporary home, and the brothers were her very devoted servants, taking her everywhere she wished to go, helping her over every difficult place, and teaching her to have such confidence in them, and such trust in their guidance, that she soon ceased to feel fear however wild was the ascent or descent, however lonely the region in which she found herself.

Although Wendot continued her favourite, and Griffeth stood next, owing to his likeness to his eldest brother, the twins soon won her favour also. They were in some respects more interesting, as they were less easily understood, wilder and stranger in their ways, and always full of stories of adventure and warfare, which fascinated her imagination even when she knew that they spoke of the strife between England and Wales. She had a high spirit and a love of adventure, which association with these stalwart boys rapidly developed.

One thing about Llewelyn and Howel gratified her childlike vanity, and gave her considerable pleasure. They would praise her agility and courage, and urge her on to make trial of her strength and nerve, when the more careful Wendot would beg her to be careful and not risk herself by too great recklessness. A few days spent in this pure, free air seemed to infuse new life into her frame, and the colour in her cheeks and the light in her eyes deepened day by day, to the motherly satisfaction of the Lady of Dynevor and the pride of Wendot, who regarded the child as his especial charge.

But in his father's absence many duties fell upon Wendot, and there came a bright evening when he and Griffeth were occupied about the castle, and only Llewelyn and Howel had leisure to wander with the little guest to her favourite spot to see the red sun set.

Llewelyn was full of talk that evening, and spoke with a rude eloquence and fire that always riveted the attention of the child. He told of the wild, lonely beauty of a certain mountain peak which he pointed out up the valley, of the

Evelyn Everett-Green

weird charm of the road thither, and above all of the eagle's nest which was to be found there, and the young eaglets being now reared therein, which he and Howel meant to capture and keep as their own, and which they purposed to visit the very next day to see if they were fit yet to leave the nest.

Gertrude sat entranced as the boy talked, and when she heard of the eagle's nest she gave a little cry of delight.

"O Llewelyn, take me with you. Let me see the eagle's nest and the little eaglets."

But the boy shook his head doubtfully.

"You could not get as far. It is a long way, and a very rough walk."

The child shook back her curling hair defiantly.

"I could do it! I know I could. I could go half the way on my palfrey, and walk the rest. You would help me. You know how well I can climb. Oh, do take me—do take me! I should so love to see an eagle's nest."

But still Llewelyn shook his head.

"Wendot would not let you go; he would say it was too dangerous."

Again came the little defiant toss.

"I am not Wendot's slave; I can do as I choose."

"If he finds out he will stop you."

"But we need not tell him, need we?"

"I thought you always told him everything."

The child stamped her little foot.

"I tell him things generally, but I can keep a secret. If he would stop us from going, we will not tell him, nor Griffeth either. We will get up very early and go by ourselves. We could do that, could we not, and come back with the young eaglets in our hands? O let us go! let us do it soon, and take me with you, kind Llewelyn! Indeed I shall not be in your way. I will be very good. And you know you have taught me to climb so well. I know I can go where you can go. You said so yourself once."

Llewelyn turned his head away to conceal a smile half of triumph, half of contempt. A strange flash was in his eyes as he looked up the valley towards the crag upon which he had told the child the eyry of the eagles hung. She thought he was hesitating still, and laid a soft little hand upon his arm.

"Please say that I may go."

He turned quickly and looked at her. For a moment she shrank back from the strange glow in his eyes; but her spirit rose again, and she said rather haughtily: "You need not be angry with me. If you don't wish me to come I will stay at home with Wendot. I do not choose to ask favours of anybody if they will not give them readily."

"I should like to take you if it would be safe," answered Llewelyn, speaking as if ashamed of his petulance or reluctance.

"Howel, could she climb to the crag where we can look

down upon the eyry if we helped her up the worst places?"

"I think she could."

The child's face flushed; she clasped her hands together and listened eagerly whilst the brothers discussed the plan which in the end was agreed to—a very early start secretly from the castle before the day dawned, the chief point to be observed beforehand being absolute secrecy, so that the projected expedition should not reach the ears either of Wendot, his mother, or Griffeth. It was to be carried out entirely by the twins themselves, with Gertrude as their companion.

CHAPTER III

THE EAGLE'S CRAG

"Where is the maid, mother?"

"Nay, I know not, my son. I thought she was with thee."

"I have not seen her anywhere. I have been busy with the men."

"Where are the other boys?"

"That I know not either. I have seen none since I rose this morning. I have been busy."

"The maid had risen and dressed herself, and had slipped out betimes," said the Lady of Dynevor, as she took her place at the board. "Methought she would be with thee. She is a veritable sprite for flitting hither and thither after thee. Doubtless she is with some of the others. Who knows where the boys have gone this morning? They are not wont to be absent at the breakfast hour."

This last question was addressed to the servants who were at the lower end of the board, and one of them spoke up in reply. By what he said it appeared that Griffeth had started off early to fly a new falcon of his, and it seemed probable that his brothers and little Lady Gertrude had accompanied him; for whilst he had been discussing with the falconer the best place for making the proposed trial, Llewelyn had been to the stables and had saddled and led out the palfrey upon which their little guest habitually rode, and there seemed no reason to doubt that all the party had gone somewhere up upon the highlands to watch the maiden essay of the bird.

"She would be sure to long to see the trial," said Wendot, attacking the viands before him with a hearty appetite. "She always loves to go with us when there is anything to see or hear. I marvel that she spoke not of it to me, but perchance it slipped her memory."

The early risers were late at the meal, but no one was anxious about them. When anything so engrossing as the flying of a young falcon was in the wind, it was natural that so sublunary a matter as breakfast should be forgotten. The servants had finished their meal, and had left the table before there was any sign of the return of the wanderers, and then it was only Griffeth who came bounding in, his face flushed and his eyes shining as he caressed the hooded bird upon his wrist.

"He is a beauty, Wendot. I would thou hadst been there to see. I took him up to—"

"Ay, tell us all that when thou hast had something to eat," said Wendot. "And where is Gertrude? she must be well-nigh famished by this time."

"Gertrude? Nay, I know not. I have not seen her. I would not have wearied her with such a tramp through the heavy dews."

"But she had her palfrey; Llewelyn led it away ere it was well light. Were you not all together?"

"Nay, I was all alone. Llewelyn and Howel were off and away before I was ready; for when I sought them to ask if they would come, they were nowhere to be found. As for the maid, I never thought of her. Where can they have taken her so early?"

A sudden look of anxiety crossed Wendot's face; but he repressed any exclamation of dismay, and glanced at his mother to see if by any chance she shared his feeling. But her face was calm and placid, and she said composedly:

"If she is with Llewelyn and Howel she will be safe. They have taken her on some expedition in secret, but none will harm her with two such stout protectors as they."

And then the lady moved away to commence her round of household duties, which in those days was no sinecure; whilst Wendot stood in the midst of the great hall with a strange shadow upon his face. Griffeth, who was eagerly discussing his breakfast, looked wonderingly at him.

"Brother, what ails thee?" he said at length; "thou seemest ill at ease."

"I am ill at ease," answered Wendot, and with a quick glance round him to assure himself that there was no one by to hear, he approached Griffeth with hasty steps and sat down beside him, speaking in a low, rapid way and in English, "Griffeth, tell me, didst thou hear aught last night ere thou fell asleep?"

"Ay, I heard Wenwynwyn singing to his harp in his own chamber, but nought beside."

"I heard that too," said Wendot, "and for his singing I could not sleep; so when it ceased not, I rose and stole to his room to ask him to forbear, yet so wild and strange was the song he sang that at the door I paused to listen; and what thinkest thou was the burden that he sang?"

"Nay, I know not; tell me."

"He sang a strange song that I have never heard before, of how a dove was borne from safe shelter—a young dove in the absence of the father bird; not the mother bird, but the father—and carried away to the eagle's nest by two fierce young eaglets untamed and untamable, there to be left till the kites come down to carry off the prize.

"Ha! thou startest and changest colour! What is it thou fearest? Where are Llewelyn and Howell and what have they done with the maid? What kuowest thou, Griffeth?"

"I know nought," answered Griffeth, "save that Wenwynwyn has been up to the commot of Llanymddyvri, and thou knowest what all they of that place feel towards the English. Then Llewelyn and Howel have been talking of late of the eagle's nest on the crag halfway thither, and if they had named it to Gertrude she would have been wild to go and see it. We know when Wenwynwyn sings his songs how he ever calls Maelgon ap Caradoc the kite, and the lords of Dynevor the eagles. But, Wendot, it could not be—a child—a maid—and our father's guest. I cannot believe it of our own brothers."

"I know not what to think, but my heart misgives me. Thou knowest what Llewelyn ever was, and Howel is but his shadow. I have mistrusted this strange friendship before now, remembering what chanced that first day, and that Llewelyn never forgives or forgets; but I would not have dreamed of such a thing as this. Yet, Griffeth, if the thing is so, there is no time to lose. I am off for the crag this very minute. Thou must quietly collect and arm a few of our stanchest men, together with the English servants left here with their young mistress. Let all be done secretly and quietly, and come after me with all speed. It may be that we are on a fool's errand, and that our fears are groundless. But truly it may be that our brothers are about to betray our guest into the hands of one of England's most bitter foes.

"Oh, methinks were her father to return, and I had her not safe to deliver back to him, I would not for very shame live to see the day when I must avow to him what had befallen his child at the hands of my brethren!"

Griffeth was fully alive to the possible peril menacing the child, and eagerly took his orders from his elder brother. It would not be difficult to summon some dozen of the armed men on the place to accompany him quietly and secretly. They would follow upon Wendot's fleet steps with as little delay as might be, and would at least track the fugitive and her guides, whether they succeeded in effecting a rescue that day or not.

Wendot waited for nothing but to give a few directions to his brother. Scarce ten minutes had elapsed from the moment when the first illumination of mind had come to him respecting some plot against the life of an innocent child, before he had armed himself, and unleashed two of the fleetest, strongest, fiercest of the hounds, and was speeding up across the moor and fell towards the lonely crag of the eagle's nest, which lay halfway between the castle of Dynevor and the abode of Maelgon ap Caradoc.

There was one advantage Wendot possessed over his brothers, and that was that he could take the wild-deer tracks

Evelyn Everett-Green

which led straight onward and upward, whilst they with their charge would have to keep to the winding mule track, which trebled the distance. The maiden's palfrey was none too clever or surefooted upon these rough hillsides, and their progress would be but slow.

Wendot moved as if he had wings to his feet, and although the hot summer sun began to beat down upon his head, and his breath came in deep, laboured gasps, he felt neither heat nor fatigue, but pressed as eagerly onwards and upwards as the strong, fleet hounds at his side.

He knew he was on the right track; for ever and anon his path would cross that which had been trodden by the feet of the boys and the horse earlier in the day, and his own quick eyes and the deep baying of the hounds told him at once whenever this was the case. Upwards and onwards, onwards and upwards, sprang the brave lad with the untiring energy of a strong and righteous purpose. He might be going to danger, he might be going to his death; for if he came into open collision with the wild and savage retainers of Maelgon, intent upon obtaining their prey, he knew that they would think little of stabbing him to the heart rather than be balked. There was no feud so far between Llanymddyvri and Dynevor, but Wendot knew that his father was suspected of leaning towards the English cause, and that it would take little to provoke some hostile demonstration on the part of his wild and reckless neighbour. The whole country was torn and rent by internecine strife, and there was a chronic state of semi-warfare kept up between half the nobles of the country against the other half.

But of personal danger Wendot thought nothing. His own honour and that of his father were at stake. If the little child left in their care were treacherously given up to the foes of the English, the boy felt that he should never lift up his head again. He must save her—he would. Far rather would he die in her defence than face her father with the story of the base treachery of his brothers.

The path grew wilder and steeper; the vegetation became more scant. The heat of the sun was tempered by the cold of the upper air. It was easier to climb, and the boy felt that his muscles were made of steel.

Suddenly a new sound struck upon his ear. It was like the whinny of a horse, only that there was in it a note of distress. Glancing sharply about him, Wendot saw Lady Gertrude's small white palfrey standing precariously on a ledge of rock, and looking pitifully about him, unable to move either up or down. The creature had plainly been turned loose and abandoned, and in trying to find his way home had stranded upon this ledge, and was frightened to move a step. Wendot was fond of all animals, and could not leave the pretty creature in such a predicament.

"Besides, Gertrude may want him again for the descent," he said; and although every moment was precious, he contrived to get the horse up the steep bank and on to better ground, and then tethered him on a small grassy plateau, where he could feed and take his ease in safety for an hour or two to come.

That matter accomplished, the lad was up and off again. He had now to trust to the hounds to direct him, for he did not know what track his brothers would have taken, and the hard rocks gave no indications which he could follow. But the dogs were well used to their work, and with their noses to the ground followed the trail unceasingly, indicating from time to time by a deep bay that they were absolutely certain of their direction.

Evelyn Everett-Green

High overhead loomed the apex of the great crag. Wendot knew that he had not much farther to go. He was able to distinguish the cairn of stones which he and his brothers had once erected on the top in honour of their having made the ascent in a marvellously short space of time. Wendot had beaten that record today, he knew; but his eyes were full of anxiety instead of triumph. He was scanning every track and every inch of distance for traces of the foe he felt certain were somewhere at hand. Had they been here already, and had they carried off the prey? Or were they only on their way, and had he come in time to thwart their purpose yet?

Ha! what was that?

Wendot had reached the shoulder of the mountain; he could see across the valley—could see the narrow winding track which led to the stronghold of Maelgon. The Eagle's Crag, as it was called, fell away precipitously on the other side. No one could scale it on that face. The path from the upper valley wound round circuitously towards it; and along this path, in the brilliant sunshine, Wendot saw distinctly the approach of a small band of armed men. Yes: they were approaching, they were not retreating. Then they had not already taken their prey; they were coming to claim it. The boy could have shouted aloud in his triumph and joy; but he held his peace, for who could tell what peril might not lie in the way?

The next moment he had scaled the steep, slippery rock which led to the precipitous edge of the crag. Not a sign could he see of his brothers or the child, but the hounds led right on to the very verge of the precipice, and for a moment the boy's heart stood still. What if they had grown afraid of the consequences of their own act, and had resolved to get rid of the child in a sure and safe fashion!

For a moment Wendot's blood ran cold. He recalled the traits of fierce cruelty which had sometimes shown themselves in Llewelyn from childhood, his well-known hatred of the English, his outburst of passion with Gertrude, so quickly followed by a strange appearance of friendship. Wendot knew his countrymen and his nation's characteristics, and knew that fierce acts of treachery were often truly charged upon them. What if—But the thought was too repellent to be seriously pursued, and shaking it off by an effort, he raised his voice and called his brothers by name.

And then, almost as it seemed from beneath his very feet, there came an answering call; but the voice was not that of his brothers, but the cry of a terrified child.

"Oh, who are you? Do, please, come to me. I am so frightened. I know I shall fall. I know I shall be killed. Do come to me quickly. I don't know where Llewelyn and Howel have gone."

"I am coming—I am Wendot," cried the boy, his heart giving a sudden bound. "You are not hurt, you are safe?"

"Yes; only so giddy and frightened, and the sun is so hot and burning, and yet it is cold, too. It is such a narrow place, and I cannot get up or down. I can't see the eagle's nest, and they have been such a long time going after it. They said they would bring the nest and the young eagles up to me, but they have never come back. I'm afraid they are killed or hurt. Oh, if you would only help me up, then we would go and look for them together! Oh, I am so glad that you have come!"

Wendot could not see the child, though every word she spoke was distinctly audible. He certainly could not reach her from the place where he now stood; but the hounds had been following the tracks of the quarry they had been scenting all this way, and stood baying at a certain spot some fifty yards away, and a little lower down than the apex of the crag. It was long since Wendot had visited this spot, his brothers knew it better than he; but when he got to the place indicated by the dogs, he saw that there was a little precipitous path along the face of the cliff, which, although very narrow and not a little dangerous, did give foothold to an experienced mountaineer. How the child had ever had the nerve to tread it he could not imagine, but undoubtedly she was there, and he must get her back, if possible, and down the mountainside, before those armed men from the upper valley could reach them.

But could he do this? He cast an apprehensive glance over his shoulder, and saw to his dismay how quickly they were approaching. From their quickened pace he fancied that his own movements had been observed. Certainly there was not a moment to lose, and leaving the dogs to keep guard at the entrance, he set his foot upon the perilous path and carefully pursued his way.

The face of the cliff jutted outwards for some yards, and then made a sharp turn round an angle. At the spot where this turn occurred, a sort of natural arch had formed itself over the narrow ledge which formed the path, and immediately behind the arch there was a small plateau which gave space to stand and move with some freedom, although a step over the edge would plunge the unwary victim into the deep gulf beneath. The cliff then fell away once again, but the ledge wound round it still, until it ended in a shallow alcove some eight feet deep, which lay just beneath the highest part of the crag, which overhung it by many yards.

And it was crouched up against the cliff in this little alcove that Wendot found Gertrude; cowering, white-faced, against the hard rock, faint from want of food, terrified at the loneliness and at her own fears for the safety of her companions, and so overwrought by the tension of nerve she had undergone, that when Wendot did stand beside her she could only cling to him sobbing passionately, and it was long before he could even induce her to let him go, or to attempt to eat the contents of a small package he had had the forethought to bring in his wallet.

He heard her tale as she sobbed in his arms. They had come here after the eagle's nest. Llewelyn and Howel had been so kind! They had not minded her being so slow, but had brought her all the way; and when she wanted to follow them along the ledge to get a better view of the nest, they had blindfolded her that she might not get giddy, and had put a rope round her and brought her safely along the narrow ledge till she had got to this place. But the nest could not be seen even from there, and they had left her to see where it really was. They said they would soon be back, but they had not come, and she had got first anxious and then terrified about them, and then fearful for her own safety. At last when faintness and giddiness had come upon her, and she could get no answer to her repeated shouts, her spirit had altogether given way; and unless Wendot had really come to her rescue, she was certain she should have fallen down the precipice. She did not know now how she should ever get back along the narrow ridge, she was so frightened and giddy. But if Llewelyn and Howel would come, perhaps she might.

Did Wendot know where they were? Would he take care of her now, and bring her safe home?

"I will if I can," answered the boy, with a strange light in his blue eyes. "Griffeth is on his way with plenty of help. He will be here soon. Do you think you could walk along the ridge now, if I were to hold you up and help you? We should get home sooner if you could."

But the child shrank back and put her hand before her eyes.

"Oh, let us wait till Griffeth comes. I am so giddy still, and I am so afraid I should fall. Hark! I'm sure I hear voices. They are coming already. Oh, I am so glad! I do want to get home. Wendot, why do you look like that? Why do you get out that thing? You are not going to fight?"

"Lady Gertrude," said Wendot, speaking in a grave, manly way that at once riveted the child's attention, "I am afraid that those voices do not belong to our friends, but to a band of men who are coming to try and take you prisoner to a castle up the valley there. No: do not be frightened; I will save you from them if I can. There is help coming for us, and I think I can hold this path against them for some time to come. You must try and keep up heart and not be frightened. You may see some hard blows struck, but you can shut your eyes and not think about it. If they do kill me and carry you off, do not give up hope, for Griffeth and our own men will be after you to rescue you. Now let me go, and try not to be afraid. I think we can hold them at bay till we are more equally matched."

The child's eyes dilated with horror. She caught Wendot by the hand.

"Give me up," she said firmly. "I will not have you killed for me. I would rather go with them. Give me up, I say!"

"No, Gertrude; I will not give you up," answered Wendot very quietly, but with an inflexibility of tone which made his voice seem like that of another person. "Your father placed you in my hands; to him I must answer for your safety. What is life to a man without honour? Would you have me stain my name for the sake of saving my life? I think not that that is the English code of honour."

Child as she was, little Gertrude understood well what was implied in those words, and a new light flashed into her eyes. Something of the soldier spirit awoke within her, and she snatched at a small dagger Wendot carried in his belt, and drawing her small figure to its full height, she said:

"We will both fight, Wendot; we will both fight, and both die rather than let them take us."

He smiled, and just for a moment laid his hand upon her head; then he drew on his mailed gloves and looked well to the buckles of the stout leathern jerkin, almost as impervious to the stabs of his foes as a suit of mail itself. The temper of his weapon he well knew; he had no fear that it would play him false. He had not the headpiece of mail; he had started in too great a hurry to arm himself completely, and speed was too much an object for him to willingly encumber himself needlessly. But as he skirted the narrow ledge, and placed himself beneath the protecting arch, he smiled grimly to himself, and thought that the stone would be as good a guard, and that here was a place where a man could sell his life dear, and send many a foe to his account before striking his own colours.

Scarcely had he well established himself in the commanding position he had resolved upon, when the sound of voices became more distinct. The party had plainly arrived at the appointed place, and Wendot could hear them discussing who was best fitted for the task of traversing the dangerous ledge to bring back the captive who was to be found there. The wild Welsh was unintelligible to Gertrude, or she would have known at once what dark treachery had been planned and carried out by her trusted companions; but Wendot's cheek glowed with shame, and he set his teeth hard, resolved to redeem the honour of his father's name to the last drop of his blood if he should be called upon to shed it in the cause.

Evelyn Everett-Green

He heard the slow and cautious steps approaching along the path, and he gripped his weapon more tightly in his hand. The red light of battle was in his eyes, and the moment he caught sight of the form of the stalwart soldier threading his perilous way along the path he sprang upon him with a cry of fury, and hurled him into the gulf beneath.

Down fell the man, utterly unprepared for such an attack, and his sharp cry of terror was echoed from above by a dozen loud voices.

Cries and shouts and questions assailed Wendot, but he answered never a word. Those above knew not if it had been an accident, or if an ambushed foe had hurled their comrade to destruction. Again came a long pause for consideration— and every moment wasted was all in favour of the pair upon the ledge—and then it became plain that some course of action had been determined upon, and Wendot heard the cautious approach of another foe. This man crept on his way much more cautiously, and the youth held himself ready for a yet more determined spring. Luckily for him, he could remain hidden until his opponent was close to him; and so soon as he was certain from the sound that the man was reaching the angle of the rock, he made another dash, and brought down his sword with all the strength of his arm upon the head of the assailant.

Once again into the heart of the abyss crashed the body of the unfortunate soldier; but a sharp thrill of pain ran through Wendot's frame, and a barbed arrow, well aimed at the joint of his leather jerkin, plunged into his neck and stuck fast.

The first assailant whom he had disposed of was but one of a close line, following each other in rapid succession. As his face became visible to the man now foremost a shout of surprise and anger rose up.

"It is Res Wendot! It is one of the sons of the house of Dynevor!

"Wendot, thou art mad! We are the friends of thy house. We are here at the instigation of thine own kindred. Give us the maid, and thou shalt go free. We would not harm thee."

"Stir but one step nearer, and I slay thee as I have slain thy two comrades," cried Wendot, in a voice which all might hear. "I deal not in treachery towards those that trust us. I will answer for the safety of the maid with mine own life. Of my hand her father will demand her when he comes again. Shall we men of Wales give right cause to the English to call us murderers, traitors, cowards? Take my life if you will, take it a thousand times over if you will, it is only over my dead body that you will reach that child."

"Down with him—traitor to the cause! He is sold to the English! He is no countryman of ours! Spare him not! He is worthy of death! Down with every Welshman who bands not with those who would uphold his country's cause!"

Such were the shouts which rent the air as the meaning of Wendot's words made itself understood. As for the brave lad himself, he had plucked the arrow from his neck, and now stood boldly on guard, resolved to husband his strength and keep on the defensive only, hoping thus to gain time until Griffeth and the armed men should arrive.

He had all the advantage of the position; but his foes were strong men, and came on thick and fast one after another, till it seemed as if the lad might be forced backwards by sheer weight and pressure. But Wendot was no novice at the use of arms: as his third foe fell upon him with heavy blows of his weighted axe, he stepped backwards a pace, and let the blows descend harmlessly upon the solid rock of the arch;

until the man, disgusted at the non-success of his endeavours to tempt his adversary out of his defended position, threw away his blunted axe, and was about to draw his sword for a thrust, when the boy sprang like lightning upon him, and buried his poniard in his heart.

Over went the man like a log, almost dragging Wendot with him as he fell, and before the youth had had time to recover himself, he had received a deep gash in his sword arm from the foe who pressed on next, and who made a quick dash to try to get possession of the vantage ground of the arch.

But Wendot staggered back as if with weakness, let his adversary dash through the arch after him; and then, hurling himself upon him as he passed through, pushed him sheer off the ledge on the other side into the yawning gulf beneath.

The comrades of this last victim, who had just sent up a shout of triumph, now changed their note, and it became a yell of rage. Wendot was back in his old vantage ground, wounded by several arrows, spent by blows, and growing faint from loss of blood, but dauntless and resolute as ever, determined to sell his life dearly, and hold out as long as he had breath left in him, sooner than let the helpless child fall into the clutches of these fierce men, goaded now to madness by the opposition they had met with.

Hark! what was that? It was a shout, a hail, and then the familiar call of the Dynevor brothers rang through the still air.

"La-ha-boo!"

It was Griffeth's voice. He had come at last. It was plain that the foe had heard, and had paused; for if they were menaced from another quarter, it was time to think of their own safety.

Summoning up all his strength, Wendot sent back an answering hail, and the next moment there was the sound of fierce voices and the clashing of weapons overhead on the summit of the cliff; and in quick, urgent accents Wendot's foes were ordered to retreat, as there was treachery somewhere, and they had been betrayed.

Wendot saw his antagonists lower their weapons, and return the way they had come, with fearful backward glances, lest their boy foe should be following them. But he had no wish to do that. He was spent and exhausted and maimed. He turned backwards towards the safer shelter of the little alcove, and sank down beside the trembling child, panting, bleeding, and almost unconscious.

Evelyn Everett-Green

CHAPTER IV

WENDOT'S REWARD

"Father, father, father!"

The shrill, glad cry broke from the lips of little Gertrude almost at the same moment as Wendot sank at her feet, spent and fainting; and the lad, making a great effort, opened his dim eyes to see the tall form of the English noble stooping over his little daughter, gathering her in his arms with a gesture of passionate endearment.

Wendot fancied he must be dreaming; perhaps it was all a strange, terrible dream: everything was swimming before his eyes in a sort of blood-coloured mist. He gave up the effort to try to disentangle the maze in which he seemed to be moving, and was sinking into unconsciousness again when a sharp cry from his brother aroused him.

"Wendot, Wendot!—O father, see—they have killed him!"

"Nay, lad, not that. Here, let me get to him.

"Griffeth, run thou and tell the fellows to let down ropes from above to draw him up. He cannot return along that narrow ledge. He and the child had best be drawn up by those above. Tell them to lose no time. The boy must be taken home to his mother's care. This narrow ledge is growing like an oven. Bid one of the men run to the brook for a draught of water."

Wendot's lips framed themselves to the word "water" as he heard it spoken. If he had but a draught of water, perhaps he could speak again and understand what was passing. As it was, he only heard the sound of a confusion of voices, the clear tones of little Gertrude being the most continuous and the most distinct. She seemed to be pouring some tale into the ears of her listeners, and Wendot was certain, from the quick, sudden movements of his father, who was supporting him as he lay, that the story heard was exciting in him feelings of indignation and amazement, although the boy's brain was too much confused to tell him the reason for this displeasure.

But the sense of rest and safety inspired by his father's presence was very comforting; and when the wounded lad had been drawn to the summit of the cliff by the strong, willing arms of the retainers, and his hurts rudely dressed by kindly hands, and his parched throat refreshed by deep draughts of cold water, he began to shake off the sense of unreality which had made him feel like one in a dream, and to marvel at the unexpected appearance on the lonely fell of his father and Lord Montacute.

A sure-footed mountain pony was bearing him gently down the steep slope, and his questioning look called Griffeth to his side.

"What means all this, Griffeth?" he whispered. "Whence came they? and what do they know? And Llewelyn and Howel, where are they? Can it be that they—"

Evelyn Everett-Green

He could not frame his lips to speak the words, but Griffeth understood him without, and his cheek flushed.

"I fear me it is indeed as we thought. She went with them, and they left her alone on the ledge, where once the eagle's eyry used to be. Maelgon's men came to carry her off thence. Had it not been for thee, Wendot, she would have been in their hands ere now. I would I had stood beside thee, brother. I would I had shared thy perils and thy hurts."

"Thou didst better than that," answered Wendot, faintly smiling, "for thou broughtest aid in the very nick of time. And how came it that our father and our guest were with thee? Methought it must surely be a dream when I saw them."

"Ay, we met them journeying towards the castle when we had but made a short mile from it. They would have reached last night but for an accident to one of the beasts, which detained them on the road; but they had started ere the sun rose, and were hard by when we encountered them. Hearing our errand, some went forward as before, but others joined our party. It was well we were thus reinforced, for Maelgon's men fight like veritable wolves."

"What knoweth our father of the matter? Spakest thou to him of Llewelyn and Howel?"

"I had perforce to do so, they questioned me so closely. I know not what they thought. Our guest's face is not one that may be read like a book, and our father only set his lips in his stern fashion, as though he would never open them again. I trow he is sore displeased that sons of his should thus act; but perchance it may not be so bad as we think."

Wendot made no reply. He was growing too spent and weary to have words or thoughts to spare. It seemed as if the long and weary descent would never be accomplished; and the beat of the sun beating down upon them mercilessly as they reached the lower ground turned him sick and faint. Little Gertrude, mounted now upon her palfrey, was chattering ceaselessly to her father, as he strode on beside her down the hillside; but Lord Montacute was grave and silent; and as for the face of Res Vychan, it looked as if carved out of marble, as he planted himself by the side of the sturdy pony who carried his son, and placed his arm round the lad to support him during that long and weary ride.

It was plain that the thoughts of both men were of a very serious complexion, and gave them food for much reflection and consideration.

Griffeth bounded on a little ahead of the cavalcade, excited by the events of the day, anxious for his brother, yet intensely proud of him, envying him the chance of thus displaying his heroic qualities, yet only wishing to have shared them—not that anything should be detracted from the halo which encircled Wendot. He had reached a turn in the path, and for a moment was alone and out of sight of the company that followed, when the hounds who had accompanied Wendot, and were now returning with them, uttered a deep bay as of welcome, and the next moment two dark and swarthy heads appeared from behind the shelter of some great boulders, and the faces of Llewelyn and Howel looked cautiously forth.

In a moment Griffeth was by their side, various emotions struggling in his face for mastery; but the tie of brotherhood was a strong one, and his first words were those of warning.

"It is all known—our father knows, and hers. I know not what your punishment will be. I have never seen our father look so stern. Do as you will about returning home, but I wot not how you will be received."

Llewelyn and Howel exchanged glances; and the former asked eagerly, "And the maid?"

"Is safe with her father and ours. Wendot risked his life to save her from Maelgon's men. Nay, linger not to hear the tale, if you would fly from the anger of those who know that you sought to betray her. It will be no easy thing to make peace with our father. You know his thoughts upon the sacredness of hospitality."

But even as he spoke Griffeth saw the change that came over his brothers' faces as they looked past him to something behind; then as he himself turned quickly to see what it was, he beheld their father and two of the servants approaching; and Res Vychan pointed sternly to the two dark-leaded boys, now involuntarily quailing beneath the fiery indignation in his eyes, and said:

"Bind them hand and foot and carry them to the castle. They shall be dealt with there as their offence shall warrant."

Then turning on his heel, he rejoined the company; whilst Llewelyn and Howel were brought captive to the paternal halls of Dynevor.

Wendot knew very little of the occurrences of the next few days. He was carried to the chamber that he shared with Griffeth, and there he lay for several days and nights in a dreamy, semi-conscious state, tended by his mother with all the skill and tenderness she possessed, and, save when the pain of his wounds made him restless and feverish, sleeping much, and troubling his head little about what went on within or without the castle. He was dimly aware that little Gertrude came in and out of his room sometimes, holding to his mother's hands, and that her gentle prattle and little caressing gestures were very soothing and pleasant. But he did not trouble his head to wonder how it was he was lying there, nor what event had crippled him so; and only in the fevered visions of the night did he see himself once again standing upon the narrow ledge of the Eagle's Crag, with a host of foes bearing down upon him to overpower and slay both him and his charge.

But after a few days of feverish lassitude and drowsiness the lad's magnificent constitution triumphed—the fever left him; and though he now lay weak and white upon his narrow bed, his mind was perfectly clear, and he was eager and anxious to know what had happened whilst he had been shut out from the life of the castle.

His mother was naturally the one to whom he turned for information. He saw that she was unwontedly pale and grave and thoughtful. As she sat beside his bed with some needlework in her hands one bright afternoon, when the sunlight was streaming into the chamber, and the air floating in through the narrow casement was full of scent and song, his eyes fixed themselves upon her face with more of purpose and reflection, and he begged her to tell him all that had passed.

"For I know that our guests are still here. Gertrude comes daily to see me. But where are Llewelyn and Howel? I have not seen them once. Is my father angry with them still? or have they been punished and forgiven?"

"Your brothers are still close prisoners," answered the mother with a sigh. "They have been chastised with more severity than any son of ours has needed to be chastised before; but they still remain sullen and obdurate and revengeful, and thy father will not permit them to come out

Evelyn Everett-Green

from their retirement so long as our guests remain. Perchance it is best so, for it would but cause trouble in the house for them to meet. I would that they could see matters differently; and yet there are many amongst our people who would say that the true patriotism was theirs."

"And our guests, mother—why linger they still? Methought they Would leave so soon as Lord Montacute returned."

"So they purposed once; but he has wished to remain till thou art sound once more, my son. He hath a very warm feeling towards thee, and would speak to thee of something that is in his heart ere he quits Dynevor. He has spoken of it to thy father and to me, but he wishes thee to hear it from his own lips."

Wendot's interest was aroused. Something in his mother's expression told him that the thing of which she spoke was a matter of some importance. As an eldest son and forward for his years, and of a reflective and thoughtful turn, he had often been consulted by his parents, and particularly by his mother, in matters rather beyond his comprehension, and had shared in discussions which many youths of his age would have shunned and despised. Now, therefore, he looked eagerly at his mother and said:

"What is it he wishes to say Canst thou not tell me thyself?"

The Lady of Dynevor paused awhile in thought; and when she spoke, it did not appear to be in direct reply to her son's question.

"Wendot," she said gravely, "thou hast heard much talk of the troubled state of these times and of the nation's affairs. Thou hast lived long enough to see how hopeless some amongst us feel it ever to hope for unity amongst ourselves.

We are torn and distracted by faction and feud. Families are banded together against families, and brothers strive with brothers for the inheritance each claims as his own. Each lord of some small territory tries to wrest from his weaker neighbour that which belongs to him; and if for a moment at some great crisis petty feuds are forgotten, and a blow is struck for national liberty, scarce has peace been proclaimed again before the old strife breaks out once more, and our fair land is desolated by a more grievous war than ever the English wage."

Wendot bent his head in voiceless assent. He knew something of his country's history, and that his mother spoke only the sad truth.

"My son," continued she after a pause, "it chances sometimes in this troubled life of ours that we are called upon to make choice, not between good and evil, but between two courses, both of which are beset with difficulties and obstacles, both of which mingle together evil and good, for which and against which much may be argued on both sides, and many things that are true be said for and against both. To some such choice as this has our poor country now come. Experience has taught us that she is incapable of uniting all her forces and of making of herself one compact, united kingdom. That course, and that alone, would be her true salvation; but that course she will not take, and failing that, she has to choose between being torn and rent by faction till she is an easy prey to the English king, who will then divide her territories amongst his own hungry and rapacious barons, or for the princes to submit to pay him the homage for their lands which he (possibly with injustice) demands, but which if paid will make of him their friend and protector, and will enable the country to live in peace and prosperity, assured that the king will support those who acknowledge him, and that he will not deprive of their ancestral rights any who will bring their homage to him, and hold their territory as it were from him. Understandest thou thus much?"

"Ay, mother, I understand it well; and though there is something in the thought that stirs my blood and sets it coursing through my veins in indignation—for I see not by what right the English king lays claim to our fair lands—still I know that conquest gives to the conqueror a right, and that if he chose to march against us with his armies, he might well find us too much weakened by our petty feuds to resist his strong veterans. And the English are not all bad. I have learned that these many days whilst our guests have been with us. I have thought at times that they would be true friends and allies, and that we might do well to copy them in many ways. In truth, if the choice lies betwixt being rent in pieces by each other and giving homage to the great Edward, who can be merciful and just, I would rather choose the latter. For there must be something grand and noble about him by what our little maid says; and to pay homage is no such hard thing. Why, does not he himself pay homage to the King of France for the lands he holds in his kingdom?"

A look of relief crossed the face of the mother as she heard these words from her first-born son. She took his hand in hers and said earnestly:

"Wendot, I am glad to hear thee speak thus, for thou art the heir of Dynevor, and upon thee much may fall some day. Thou knowest what thy brothers are—I speak of Llewelyn and Howel. I cannot but fear for them—unless, indeed, the rapacious greed I sometimes see in Llewelyn proves stronger than his fierce hatred to the English, and he prefers to do homage for his lands rather than lose them. But thou art the head of the family, and the chief power will rest with thee when thy father is gone. I counsel thee, if the time comes when thou must make thy choice, be not led away by blind hatred of the English. They may prove less cruel foes than thine own countrymen are to one another. If Wales may not be united under one native king, let her think well ere she rejects the grace held out to all who will yield fealty to the English monarch. That is what I wished to say to thee. Remember that the English are not always cruel, always rapacious. There are generous, noble, honourable men amongst them, of whom I am sure our guest is one."

"Ay, he has a grand face," said Wendot. "A face one can both love and trust. And all that the little one tells me of the king and his family inclines my heart towards him and his. I will remember what you have said, mother, and will ponder your words. Methinks it is no lovely thing to hate as Llewelyn and Howel hate; it makes men act rather as fiends than as honourable soldiers should."

The conversation ended there, and was not renewed; but the very next day Lord Montacute sought Wendot's room, when the lad was lying alone, wearying somewhat of his own company, and the light sprang into his eyes as he saw the guest approach, for in his own boyish way he had a great admiration for this man.

"Well, lad, I am glad to see thee looking something more substantial and like thine own self," said Lord Montacute, seating himself upon the edge of the bed and taking Wendot's hand in his. "This hand has done good service to me and mine—good service, indeed, to the King of England, who would have been forced to chastise with some severity the outrage planned upon a subject of his, and one dear to him from association with his children. Tell me, boy, what can I do for thee when I tell this tale to my lord of England? What boon hast thou to ask of him or of me? For thou needest not fear; whatever it be it shall be granted."

Evelyn Everett-Green

"Nay, I have no boon," answered Wendot, his cheek flushing. "I did but do my duty by any guest beneath my father's roof. I was responsible for the safety of the maid. I had taken that duty on myself. I want nothing; she is safe, and that is enough. Only if you would speak to my father for my brothers Llewelyn and Howel. I know they have merited deep displeasure; yet they are but lads, and doubtless they were led away by evil counsels. He would hear pleading better from you than from me."

"It shall be done," said Lord Montacute, still regarding Wendot steadily; "and now, boy, I would speak to thee seriously and gravely as man to man, for thou hast proved thyself to be a man in action, in courage, and in foresight. And thy parents tell me that thou art acquainted with the burning questions of the day, and that thy brothers' headstrong hatreds and prejudices do not blind thee."

Wendot made no reply, but fixed his bright eyes steadily on Lord Montacute's face. He on his side, after a brief silence, began again in clear, terse phrases:

"Lad, if thou livest thou wilt some day be Lord of Dynevor—master of this fair heritage, the fairest, perhaps, in all South Wales. Thou hast noble blood in thy veins—the blood of princes and kings; thou hast much that men covet to call their own; but thou art surrounded by foes who are jealous of thee, and by kinsmen who have already cast covetous eyes on thy possessions."

"Ay, that traitorous Meredith ap Res, whose mother is English, and who would—But pardon me. I would not willingly speak against your nation. Indeed, I feel not bitter as others do; only—"

"Boy, thou art right to be loyal and true. I like thee none the less for the patriotic fervour which breaks out in thee. But I am glad that thou shouldest see both sides of this matter, that thou shouldest see the peril menacing thy brothers from thine own kinsman, who has strengthened himself by an English alliance. It is useless to blind thine eyes to what is coming. They tell me thou art not blind; and I come to thee, lad, because I think well of thee, to ask if it would please thee to strengthen thy position in thine own land and in Edward's sight by an alliance with an English maiden of noble birth. Hast thou ever thought of such a thing?"

Wendot's wide-open eyes gave answer enough. Lord Montacute smiled slightly as he said:

"Ah, thou art full young for such thoughts; and thou livest not in the atmosphere of courts, where babes are given in marriage almost from their cradles. But listen, Res Wendot; I speak not in jest, I am a man of my word. Thou hast risked thy life to save my little maid. Thou art a noble youth, and I honour both thee and thy parents. The maid has told me that she loves thee well, and would be well pleased to wed thee when she is of the age to do so. These are but childish words, yet they may prove themselves true in days to come. It is in the interests of all those who have the peace and prosperity of this land at heart to strengthen themselves in every way they can. My little daughter will have an ample dower to bring her husband; and I will keep her for thee if thou wilt be willing to claim her in days to come. I should like well to see her ruling in these fair halls; and thou hast proved already that thou art a knightly youth, whose hand she may well take with confidence and pride.

"Thy parents are willing; it waits only for thee to say. What thinkest thou of a troth plight with the little maid?"

Wendot's face glowed with a sort of boyish shame, not

unmingled with pride; but the idea was altogether too strange and new to him to be readily grasped.

"I have never thought of such things," he said shyly, "and I am too young to wed. Perchance I may grow into some rough, uncouth fellow, who may please not the maiden when she reaches years of discretion. Methinks it would scarce be fair to plight her now, at least not with such a plight as might not be broken. If our nations meet in fierce conflict, as they yet may, it would be a cruel thing to have linked her hand with that of a rebel, for such we are called by the English monarch, they say, when we rise to fight for our liberties bequeathed by our ancestors.

"Nay, noble lord, frown not on me. There be moments when methinks two spirits strive within me, and I am fearful of trusting even myself. I would not that grief or sorrow should touch her through me. Let me come and claim her anon, when I have grown to man's estate, and can bring her lands and revenues. But bind her not to one whose fate may be beset with perils and shadows. There be those amongst our bards who see into the future; and they tell us that a dark fate hangs over the house of Dynevor, and that we four shall be the last to bear the name."

Lord Montacute was looking grave and earnest. There was something in his face which indicated disappointment, but also something that spoke of relief. Possibly he himself had offered this troth plight with something of hesitation, offered it out of gratitude to the noble lad, and out of respect to his parents, who, as he saw, would prove valuable allies to the English cause, could they but be induced to give their allegiance to it. Yet there was another side to the picture, too; and Wendot was too young for any one to predict with certainty what would be his course in the future. The hot blood of his race ran in his veins; and though his judgment was cool, and he saw things in a reasonable and manly light, it would be rash to predict what the future might have in store for him.

"Well, lad, thou hast spoken bravely and well," said the Englishman, after a pause for thought. "Perchance thy words are right; perchance it will be well to let matters rest as they are for the present. We will have no solemn troth plight betwixt ye twain; but the maid shall be promised to none other these next four years, so that if thou carest to claim her ere she reaches woman's estate, thou shalt find her waiting for thee. And now I must say thee farewell, for tomorrow we ride away the way we came. I trust to see thee at the king's court one of these days, and to make known to his royal majesty the noble youth of Dynevor."

Wendot was left alone then for some time, pondering the strange offer made to him, and wondering whether he had been foolish to refuse the promised reward. He had never seriously thought of marriage, although in those days wedlock was entered upon very young if there were any advantage to be gained from it. A lad of fifteen is seldom sentimental; but Wendot was conscious of a very warm spot in his heart for little Gertrude, and he knew that he should miss her sorely when she went, and think of her much. Would it have been a sweet or a bitter thing to have felt himself pledged to a daughter of England? He felt that he could not tell; but at least the decision was made now, and his words could not be recalled.

Just ere the sun set that summer's day there came down the stone corridor which led to his room the patter of little feet, and he leaned up on his elbow with brightening eyes as the door opened and little Gertrude came dancing in.

"I thought I was to have been married to you, Wendot, before

Evelyn Everett-Green

we went away," she said, looking into his face with the most trusting expression in her soft dark eyes; "but father says you will come to marry me some day at the king's court. Perhaps that will be better, for I should like Eleanor and Joanna to see you. They would like you so, and you would like them. But do come soon, Wendot. I do so like you; and I shall want to show you to them all. And I have broken my gold coin in two—the one the king gave me once. I got the armourer to do it, and to make a hole in each half. You must wear one half round your neck, and I will wear the other. And that will be almost the same as being married, will it not? And you will never forget me, will you?"

Wendot let her hang the half of the coin round his neck by a silken thread, strange new thoughts crowding into his mind as he felt her soft little hands about him. Suddenly he clasped them in both of his and pressed warm kisses upon them. Gertrude threw her arms about his neck in a childish paroxysm of affection, saying as she did so between her kisses:

"Now, it's just like being husband and wife; and we shall never forget one another—never."

CHAPTER V

THE KING'S CHILDREN

"Dynevor—did you say Dynevor? O Eleanor, it must be he!"

A tall, slim, fair-faced maiden, with a very regal mien, looked up quickly from an embroidery frame over which she was bending, and glanced from the eager, flushed face of the younger girl who stood beside her to that of a tall and stalwart English youth, who appeared to be the bearer of a piece of news, and asked in her unconsciously queenly way:

"What is it, Sir Godfrey, that you have told this impetuous child, to have set her in such a quiver of excitement?"

"Only this, gracious lady, that certain youthful chieftains from the south have come hither to Rhuddlan to pay their homage to your royal father. In his absence at Chester they have been lodged within the castle walls, as becomes their station. It has been told me that amongst them are four sons of one Res Vychan, lately dead, and that he was Lord of Dynevor, which honour has descended to his eldest son. I was telling what I knew to Lady Gertrude when she broke away to speak to you."

"Eleanor, it must be he—it must be they!" cried Gertrude,

with flushing cheek and kindling eye—"Res Vychan, Lord of Dynevor, and his four sons. It could be none else than they. O Eleanor, sweet Eleanor, bid them be brought hither to see us! Thou hast heard the story of how we went thither, my father and I, two years agone now, and of what befell me there. I have never heard a word of Wendot since, and I have thought of him so oft. Thou art mistress here now; they all heed thy lightest word. Bid that the brothers be brought hither to us. I do so long to see them again!"

Gertrude was fairly trembling with excitement; but that was no unusual thing for her, as she was an ardent, excitable little mortal, and ever in a fever of some kind or another. The young knight who had brought the news looked at her with unmistakable admiration and pleasure, and seemed as though he would gladly have obeyed any behest of hers; but he was fain to wait for the decision of the stately Eleanor, the king's eldest and much-beloved child, who in the temporary absence of her parents occupied a position of no little importance in the household, and whose will, in the royal apartments at any rate, was law.

But there were other listeners to Gertrude's eager words. At the far end of the long gallery, which was occupied by the royal children as their private apartment, a group of three young things had been at play, but the urgency of Gertrude's tones had arrested their attention, and they had drawn near to hear her last words. One of these younger children was a black-eyed girl, with a very handsome face and an imperious manner, which gave to onlookers the idea that she was older than her years. Quick tempered, generous, hasty, and self willed was the Lady Joanna, the second daughter of the king; but her warm affections caused all who knew her to love her; and her romantic temperament was always stirred to its depths by any story that savoured of chivalry or heroism.

"What!" she cried; "is Wendot here—Wendot of Dynevor, who held the Eagle's Crag against half a hundred foemen to save thee, sweetest Gertrude, from captivity or death?— Eleanor, thou knowest the story; thou must bid him hither at once! Why, I would thank him with my own lips for his heroism. For is not Gertrude as our own sister in love?"

"Ay, Eleanor, bid him come," pleaded Alphonso, a fragile-looking boy a year younger than Joanna, whose violet-blue eyes and fair skin were in marked contrast to her gipsy-like darkness of complexion; and this request was echoed eagerly by another boy, a fine, bold-looking lad, somewhat older than Alphonso, by name Britten, who was brought up with the king's children, and treated in every way like them, as the wardrobe rolls of the period show, though what his rank and parentage were cannot now be established, as no mention of him occurs in any other documents of that time.

The Princess Eleanor, as she would now be called, although in those far-back days the title of Lady was generally all that was bestowed upon the children of the king, did not attempt to resist the combined entreaties of her younger playfellows. Indeed, although somewhat mature both in mind and appearance for her years, she was by no means devoid of childish or feminine curiosity, and was as willing to see the hero of Gertrude's oft-told tale as her more youthful companions could be. Moreover, it was her father's policy and pleasure to be generous and gracious towards all those who submitted themselves to his feudal sovereignty; and to the young he ever showed himself friendly and even paternal. The stern soldier-king was a particularly tender and loving father, and his wife the best of mothers, so that the family tie in their household was a very strong and beautiful thing. When the monarch was called away from his own royal residences to quell sedition or rebellion in this turbulent country of Wales, his wife and children

Evelyn Everett-Green

accompanied him thither; and so it happened that in this rather gloomy fastness in North Wales, when the rebellion of the warlike Llewelyn had but just been crushed, the king's children were to be found assembled within its walls, by their bright presence and laughter-loving ways making the place gay and bright, and bringing even into political matters something of the leniency and good fellowship which seems to be the prerogative of childhood.

Thus it was that one powerful and turbulent noble, Einon ap Cadwalader, had left as hostage of his good faith his only child, the Lady Arthyn, to be the companion of the king's daughters. She had been received with open arms by the warm-hearted Joanna, and the two were fast friends already, although the Welsh girl was several years the elder of the pair. But Joanna, who had been educated in Spain by her grandmother and namesake, and who had only recently come to be with her own parents, had enjoyed abroad a liberty and importance which had developed her rapidly, and her mind was as quick and forward as her body was active and energetic.

Intercourse with Arthyn, too, had given to the younger princess a great sympathy with the vanquished Welsh, and she was generously eager that those who came to pay homage to her father should not feel themselves in a position that was humiliating or galling. The gentle Eleanor shared this feeling to the full, and was glad to give to the young knight Sir Godfrey Challoner, who was one of her own gentlemen-in-waiting, a gracious message for the young Lord of Dynevor to the effect that she would be glad to receive him and his brothers in her father's absence, and to give them places at the royal table for the evening meal shortly to be served.

Great was the delight of Gertrude when the message was

despatched. Her companions crowded round her to hear again the story of her adventure on the Eagle's Crag. Gertrude never knew how she had been betrayed by Wendot's brothers. She believed that they had been accidentally hindered from coming to her rescue by the difficulties of the climb after the eagle's nest. There was a faint, uncomfortable misgiving in her mind with regard to the black-browed twins, but it did not amount to actual suspicion, far less to any certainty of their enmity; and although Eleanor had heard the whole story from her parents, she had not explained the matter more fully to Gertrude.

An invitation from royalty was equal to a command, and the eager children were not kept waiting long. The double doors at the end of the long gallery, which had closed behind the retiring form of Godfrey, opened once again to admit him, and closely in his wake there followed two manly youths— two, not four—upon whose faces every eye was instantly fixed in frank and kindly scrutiny.

Wendot had developed rapidly during these two last years, although he retained all his old marked characteristics. The waving hair was still bright and sunny, the open face, with its rather square features, was resolute, alert, manly, and strong. The fearless blue eyes had not lost their far-away dreaminess, as though the possessor were looking onward and outward beyond the surroundings visible to others; and beneath the calm determination of the expression was an underlying sweetness, which shone out from time to time in the sunny smile which always won the heart of the beholder. The figure was rather that of a man than a lad—tall, strongly knit, full of grace and power; and a faint yellow moustache upon the upper lip showed the dawn of manhood in the youth. There was something in his look which seemed to tell that he had known sorrow, trial, and anxiety; but this in no way detracted from the power or attractiveness of the countenance, but rather gave it an added charm.

Griffeth retained his marked likeness to his brother, and was almost his equal in height; but his cheek was pale and hollow, while Wendot's was brown and healthy, his hands were slim and white, and there was an air of languor and ill-health about him which could not fail to make itself observed. He looked much younger than his brother, despite his tall stature, and he blushed like a boy as he saw the eyes of the ladies fixed upon them as they came forward, bowing with no ungraceful deference.

"Wendot, Wendot. don't you know me?"

The young man started and raised his eyes towards the speaker. So far, he had only been aware that there were a number of persons collected at the upper end of the long gallery. Now he found himself confronted by a pair of eager, dancing eyes, as soft and dark as those of a forest deer, whilst two slim hands were held out to him, and a silvery voice cried softly and playfully:

"O Wendot, Wendot, to think you have forgotten!"

"Lady Gertrude!"

"Ah, I am glad you have not forgotten, though methinks I have changed more than you these past years. I should have known you anywhere. But come, Wendot; I would present you to my friends and companions, who would fain be acquainted with you. They know how you saved my life that day, I have told the tale so oft.

"Let me present you first to our sweetest Lady Eleanor, our great king's eldest daughter. You will love her, I know— none can help it. And she lets me call myself her sister."

Young things have a wonderful faculty of growing intimate in a very brief space, and the formalities of those simpler times were not excessive, especially away from the trammels of the court. In ten minutes' time Wendot and his brother had grasped the names and rank of all those to whom they had been presented, and were joining in the eager talk with ease and with enjoyment. Joanna stood beside Wendot, listening, with unfeigned interest, to his answers respecting himself and those near and dear to him; whilst Alphonso had drawn Griffeth to the embrasure of a window, and was looking up into his face as they compared notes and exchanged ideas. It seemed from the first as though a strong link formed itself between those two.

"Your brothers would not come. Was that fear or shame or pride?" asked Joanna, with a laughing look into Wendot's flushed face. "Nay, think not that we would compel any to visit us who do it not willingly. Gertrude has prepared us to find your brothers different from you. Methinks she marvelled somewhat that they had come hither at all with their submission."

Wendot hesitated, and the flush deepened on his face; but he was too young to have learned the lesson of reticence, and there was something in the free atmosphere of this place which prompted him to frankness.

"I myself was surprised at it," he said. "Llewelyn and Howel have not been friendly in their dealings with the English so far, and we knew they aided Llewelyn of North Wales in the revolt which has been lately quelled. But since our parents died we have seen but little of them. They became joint owners of the commot of Iscennen, and removed from Dynevor to the castle of Carregcennen in their own territory, and until we met them some days since in company with our kinsman Meredith ap Hes, coming to tender their homage, as

Evelyn Everett-Green

we ourselves are about to do, we knew not what to think of them or what action they would take."

"Are both your parents dead, then?" asked Gertrude, with sympathy in her eyes. "I heard that Res Vychan was no longer living, but I knew not that the gentle Lady of Dynevor had passed away also."

Wendot's face changed slightly as he answered:

"They both died within a few days of each other the winter after you had been with us, Lady Gertrude. We were visited by a terrible sickness that year, and our people sickened and died in great numbers. Our parents did all they could for them, and first my father fell ill and died, and scarce had the grave closed over him before our mother was stricken, and followed him ere a week had passed. Griffeth was also lying at the point of death, and we despaired of his life also; but he battled through, and came back to us from the very gates of the grave, and yet methinks sometimes that he has never been the same since. He shoots up in height, but he cannot do the things he did when he was two years younger.

"What think you of him, sweet Lady Gertrude? Is he changed from what he was when last you saw him, ere the sickness had fastened upon him?"

Several eyes were turned towards the slim, tall figure of the Welsh lad leaning against the embrasure of the window. The sunlight fell full upon his face, showing the sharpness of its outlines, the delicate hectic colouring, the tracery of the blue veins beneath the transparent skin. And just the same transparent look was visible in the countenance of the young Prince Alphonso, who was talking with the stranger youth, and more hearts than that of Wendot felt a pang as their owners' eyes were turned upon the pair beside the sunny window. But Wendot pressed for no answer to his question, nor did Gertrude volunteer it; she only asked quickly:

"Then Griffeth and you live yet at Dynevor, beautiful Dynevor, and Llewelyn and Howel elsewhere?"

"Ay, at Carregcennen. We have our respective lands, though we are minors yet; and our kinsman Meredith ap Res is our guardian, though it is little we see of him."

"Meredith ap Res! I know him well," cried a girlish voice, in accents which betrayed her Welsh origin. "He has ever been a traitor to his country, a traitor to all who trust him; a covetous, grasping man, who will clutch at what he can get, and never cease scheming after lands and titles so long as the breath remains in him."

They all turned to see who had spoken, and Arthyn—the headstrong, passionate, patriotic Arthyn, who, despite her love for her present companions, bitterly resented being left a hostage in the hands of the English king—stood out before them, and spoke in the fearless fashion which nobody present resented.

"Wendot of Dynevor, if you are he, beware of that man, and bid your brothers beware of him, too. I know him; I have heard much of him. Be sure he has an eye on your fair lands, and he will embroil you yet with the English king if he can, that he may lay claim to your patrimony. He brings you here to the court to make your peace, to pay your homage. If I mistake not the man, you will not all of you return whence you came. He will poison the king's mind. Some traitorous practices will be alleged against you. Your lands will be withheld. You will be fed with promises which will never be fulfilled. And the kinsman who has sold himself body and soul to the English alliance will rule your lands, in your

Evelyn Everett-Green

names firstly perchance, until his power is secure, and he can claim them boldly as his own. See if it be not so."

"It shall not be so," cried Alphonso, suddenly advancing a step forward and planting himself in the midst of the group.

His cheek was crimson now, there was fire in his eyes. He had all the regal look of his royal father as he glanced up into Wendot's face and spoke with an authority beyond his years.

"I, the king's son, give you my word of honour that this thing shall not be. You are rightful Lord of Dynevor. You took not up arms against my father in the late rebellion; you come at his command to pay your homage to him. Therefore, whatever may be his dealings with your brothers who have assisted the rebels, I pledge my princely word that you shall return in peace to your own possessions. My father is a just and righteous king, and I will be his surety that he will do all that is right and just by you, Wendot of Dynevor."

"Well spoken, Alphonso!" cried Joanna and Britton in a breath, whilst Wendot took the hand extended to him, and bent over it with a feeling of loyal gratitude and respect.

There was something very lovable in the fragile young prince, and he seemed to win the hearts of all who came within the charm of his personal presence. He combined his father's fearless nobility with his mother's sweetness of disposition. Had he lived to ascend the throne of England, one of the darkest pages of its annals might never have been written.

But this hot discussion was brought to an end by the appearance of the servants, who carried in the supper, laying it upon a long table at the far end of the gallery. No great state was observed even in the royal household, when the family was far away from the atmosphere of the court as it was held at Westminster or Windsor.

A certain number of servants were in attendance. There were a few formalities gone through in the matter of tasting of dishes served to the royal children, but they sat round the table without ceremony; and when the chaplain had pronounced a blessing, which was listened to reverently by the young people, who were all very devout and responsive to religious influences, the unconstrained chatter began again almost at once, and the Welsh lads lost all sense of strangeness as they sat at the table of the king's children.

"Our father and mother will not return for several days yet," said Joanna to Wendot, whom she had placed between herself and Gertrude; "but we have liberty to do what we wish and to go where we like.

"Say, Gertrude, shall we tell Wendot on what we have set our hearts? It may be he would help us to our end."

"I would do anything you bid me, gracious lady," answered Wendot with boyish chivalry.

The girls were eying each other with flushed faces, their voices were lowered so that they should not reach the ears of the Lady Edeline, Joanna's governess, who was seated at the board, although she seldom spoke unless directly addressed by Eleanor, who seemed to be on friendly terms with her.

"Wendot," whispered Joanna cautiously, "have you ever hunted a wolf in your mountains?"

"Ay, many a time, though they be more seldom seen now. But we never rid ourselves altogether of them, do as we will."

"And have you killed one yourself?"

"Yes, I have done that, too."

"And is it very dangerous?"

"I scarce know; I never thought about it. I think not, if one is well armed and has dogs trained to their duties."

Joanna's eyes were alight with excitement; her hands were locked together tightly. Her animated face was set in lines of the greatest determination and happiest anticipation.

"Wendot," she said, "there is a wolf up yonder in that wild valley we can see from yon window, as you look towards the heights of Snowdon. Some of our people have seen and tracked it, but they say it is an old and wily one, and no one has got near it yet. Wendot, we have set our hearts on having a wolf hunt of our very own. We do not want all the men and dogs and the stir and fuss which they would make if we were known to be going. I know what that means. We are kept far away behind everybody, and only see the dead animal after it has been killed miles away from us. We want to be in the hunt ourselves—Britten, Alphonso, Arthyn, Gertrude, and I. Godfrey would perhaps be won over if Gertrude begged him, and I know Raoul Latimer would—he is always ready for what turns up—but that would not be enough. O Wendot, if you and your brothers would but come, we should be safe without anybody else. Raoul has dogs, and we could all be armed, and we would promise to be very careful. We could get away early, as Gertrude did that day she slipped off to the Eagle's Crag.

"Wendot, do answer—do say you will come. You understand all about hunting, even hunting wolves. You are not afraid?"

Wendot smiled at the notion. He did not entirely understand that he was requested to take part in a bit of defiant frolic which the young princes and princesses were well aware would not have been permitted by their parents. All he grasped was that the Lady Joanna requested his assistance in a hunt which she had planned, and with the details of which he was perfectly familiar, and he agreed willingly to her request, not sorry, either for his own sake or for that of his more discontented brothers, that the monotony of the days spent in waiting the return of the king should be beguiled by anything so attractive and exciting as a wolf hunt.

The Dynevor brothers had often hunted wolves before, and saw no special peril in the sport; and Joanna and Gertrude felt that not even the most nervous guardian could hesitate to let them go with such a stout protector.

"I do like him, Gertrude," said Joanna, when Wendot and his brother had retired. "I hope if I ever have to marry, as people generally do, especially if they are king's daughters, that I shall find somebody as brave and handsome and knightly as your Wendot of Dynevor."

For Gertrude and Joanna both took the view that the breaking of the king's gold coin between them was equivalent to the most solemn of troth plights.

CHAPTER VI

WELSH WOLVES

The Princess Joanna was accustomed to a great deal of her own way. She had been born at Acre, whilst her parents had been absent upon Edward's Crusade, and for many years she had remained in Castile with her grandmother-godmother, who had treated her with unwise distinction, and had taught her to regard herself almost as a little queen. The high-spirited and self-willed girl had thus acquired habits of independence and commanding ways which were perhaps hardly suited to her tender years; but nevertheless there was something in her bright vivacity and generous impetuosity which always won the hearts of those about her, and there were few who willingly thwarted her when her heart was set upon any particular thing.

There were in attendance upon the king and his children a number of gallant youths, sons of his nobles, who were admitted to pleasant and easy intercourse with the royal family; so that when Joanna and Alphonso set their hearts upon a private escapade of their own, in the shape of a wolf hunt, it was not difficult to enlist many brave champions in the cause quite as eager for the danger and the sport as the royal children themselves. Joanna was admitted to be a privileged person, and Alphonso, as the only son of the king, had a certain authority of his own.

The graver and more responsible guardians of the young prince and princesses might have hesitated before letting them have their way in this matter; but Joanna took counsel of the younger and more ardent spirits by whom she was surrounded, and a secret expedition to a neighbouring rocky fastness was soon planned, which expedition, by a little diplomacy and management, could be carried out without exciting much remark.

The king and queen encouraged their family in hardy exercises and early hours. If the royal children planned an early ride through the fresh morning air, none would hinder their departure, and they could easily shake off their slower attendants when the time came, and join the bolder comrades who would be waiting for them with all the needful accoutrements for the hunt on which their minds were bent.

One or two of the more youthful and adventurous attendants might come with them, but the soberer custodians might either be dismissed or outridden. They were accustomed to the vagaries of the Lady Joanna, and would not be greatly astonished at any freak on her part.

And thus it came about that one clear, cold, exhilarating morning in May, when the world was just waking from its dewy sleep of night, that Joanna and Alphonso, together with Gertrude and Arthyn, and young Sir Godfrey and another gentleman in attendance, drew rein laughingly, after a breathless ride across a piece of wild moorland, at the appointed spot, where a small but well-equipped company was awaiting them with the spears, the dogs, and the long, murderous-looking hunting knives needed by those who follow the tracks of the wild creatures of the mountains.

This little band numbered in its ranks the four Dynevor brothers; a tall, rather haughty-looking youth, by name Raoul Latimer; and one or two more with whose names we have no concern. Britten, who accompanied the royal party, sprang forward with a cry of delight at seeing the muster, and began eagerly questioning Raoul as to the capabilities of the dogs he had brought, and the possible dangers to be encountered in the day's sport.

Gertrude and Joanna rode up to Wendot and greeted him warmly. They had seen him only once since the first evening after his arrival, and both girls stole curious glances at the dark faces of the two brothers unknown as yet to them. They were almost surprised that the twins had come at all, as they were not disposed to be friendly towards the English amongst whom they were now mingling; but here they were, and Gertrude greeted both with her pretty grace, and they answered her words of welcome with more courtesy than she had expected to find in them.

Llewelyn and Howel were submitting themselves to the inevitable with what grace they could, but with very indignant and hostile feelings hidden deep in their hearts. Their old hatred towards the English remained unaltered. They would have fought the foe tooth and nail to the last had they been able to find allies ready to stand by them. But when their uncle of North Wales had submitted, and all the smaller chieftains were crowding to the court to pay homage, and when they knew that nothing but their own nominal subjection would save them from being deprived of their lands, which would go to enrich the rapacious Meredith ap Res, then indeed did resistance at that time seem hopeless; and sooner than see themselves thus despoiled by one who was no better than a vassal of England, they had resolved to take the hated step, and do homage to Edward for their lands. Indeed, these brothers had to do even more; for, having been concerned in the late rebellion, they had forfeited their claim upon their property, only that it was Edward's policy to restore all lands the owners of which submitted themselves to his authority. The brothers felt no doubt as to the result of their submission, but the humiliation involved was great, and it was hard work to keep their hatred of the English in check. Those wild spirits had not been used to exercising self-control, and the lesson came hard now that they were springing up towards man's estate, with all the untempered recklessness and heat of youth still in their veins.

Perhaps there was something in the expression of those two dark faces that told its tale to one silent spectator of the meeting between the Welsh and English; for as the party united forces and pushed onwards and upwards towards the wild ravine where the haunt of the wolf lay, the twin brothers heard themselves addressed in their own language, and though the tones were sweet and silvery, the words had a ring of passionate earnestness in them which went straight to their hearts.

"Methinks I am not mistaken in you, sons of Dynevor. You have not willingly left your mountain eyry for these halls where the proud foeman holds his court and sits in judgment upon those who by rights are free as air. I have heard of you before, Llewelyn and Howel ap Res Vychan. You are not here, like your brethren, half won over to the cause of the foe; you would fight with the last drop of your blood for the liberty of our country."

Turning with a start, the brothers beheld the form of a slight and graceful maiden, who was pushing her palfrey up beside them. She appeared to be about their own age, and was very beautiful to look upon, with a clear, dark skin, large, bright eyes, now glowing with the enthusiasm so soon kindled in the breast of the children of an oppressed people—a people

Evelyn Everett-Green

thrilling with the strange, deep poetry of their race, which made much amends for their lack of culture in other points.

Llewelyn and Howel, learning caution by experience, scarce knew how to respond to this appeal; but the girl met their inquiring glances by a vivid smile, and said:

"Nay, fear me not. I am one of yourselves—one of our country's own children. Think not that I am here of my own free will. I deny not that I have learned to love some amongst our conqueror's children and subjects, but that does not make me forget who I am nor whence I have come. Let us talk together of our country and of the slender hopes which yet remain that she may gird herself up and make common cause against the foe. Oh, would that I might live to see the day, even though my life might pay the forfeit of my father's patriotism. Let Edward slay me—ay, and every hostage he holds in his hand—so that our country shakes off the foreign yoke, and unites under one head as one nation once again."

These words kindled in the breast of the twin brothers such a glow of joy and fervour as they had not known for many a weary day. They made room for Arthyn to ride between them, and eager were the confidences exchanged between the youthful patriots as they pursued their way upwards. Little they heeded the black looks cast upon them by Raoul Latimer, as he saw Arthyn's eager animation, and understood how close was the bond which had thus quickly been established between them and the proud, silent girl whose favours he had been sedulously trying to win this many a day.

Raoul Latimer was a youth with a decided eye to the main chance. He knew that Arthyn was her father's heiress, and that she would succeed at his death to some of the richest lands in Wales. Possibly her father might be deprived of these lands in his lifetime, as he was a turbulent chieftain, by no means submissive to Edward's rule. If that were the case, and if his daughter had wedded a loyal Englishman of unquestionable fidelity, there would be an excellent chance for that husband of succeeding to the broad lands of Einon ap Cadwalader before many years had passed. Therefore young Raoul paid open court to the proud Welsh maiden, and was somewhat discomfited at the small progress he had made.

But he was a hot-headed youth, and had no intention of being thrown into the shade by any beggarly Welshmen, be they sons of Dynevor or no, so that when the party were forced by the character of the ground to dismount from their horses and take to their own feet, he pressed up to Arthyn and said banteringly:

"Sweet lady, why burden yourself with the entertainment of these wild, uncivilized loons? Surely those who can but speak the language of beasts deserve the treatment of beasts. It is not for you to be thus—"

But the sentence was never finished. Perhaps the flash from Arthyn's eye warned him he had gone too far in thus designating the youths, who were, after all, her countrymen; but there was a better reason still for this sudden pause, for Llewelyn's strong right hand had flown out straight from the shoulder, and Raoul had received on the mouth a stinging blow which had brought the red blood upon his lips and the crimson tide of fury into his cheeks.

With an inarticulate cry of rage he drew his dagger and sprang upon the young Welshman. Swords were drawn in those days only too readily, and in this case there had been provocation enough on both sides to warrant bloodshed. The youths were locked at once in fierce conflict, striking madly at each other with their shining blades, before those who stood by well knew what had occurred.

It was only too common at such times that there should be collision between the sons of England and Wales; and the suffering and the penalty almost invariably fell upon the latter. This fact was well known to the children of the king, and possibly prompted the young Alphonso to his next act.

Drawing the small sword he always carried at his side, he threw himself between the combatants, and striking up their blades he cried in tones of such authority as only those can assume who feel the right is theirs:

"Put up your weapons, gentlemen; I command you in the king's name."

"Raoul, this is your doing, I warrant. Shame on you for thus falling upon my father's guest in his absence, and he a stranger and an alien! Shame on you, I say!"

But scarce had these words been uttered before a shrill cry broke from several of the girls, who were watching the strange scene with tremulous excitement. For young Llewelyn, maddened and blinded by the heat of his passion, and not knowing either who Alphonso was or by what right he interposed betwixt him and his foe, turned furiously upon him, and before any one could interpose, a deep red gash in the boy's wrist showed what the Welsh lad's blade had done.

Wendot, Griffeth, and Godfrey flung themselves upon the mad youth, and held him back by main force. In Raoul's eyes there was an evil light of triumph and exultation.

"Llewelyn, Llewelyn, art mad? It is the king's son," cried Wendot in their native tongue; whilst Joanna sprang towards her brother and commenced binding up the gash, the lad never for a moment losing his presence of mind, or forgetting in the smart of the hurt the dignity of his position.

Llewelyn's fierce burst of passion had spent itself, and the sense of Wendot's words had come home to him. He stood shamefaced and sullen, but secretly somewhat afraid; whilst Arthyn trembled in every limb, and if looks would have annihilated, Raoul would not have existed as a corporate being a moment longer.

"Gentlemen," said Alphonso, turning to those about him, and holding up his bandaged hand, "this is the result of accident—pure accident. Remember that, if it ever comes to the ears of my father. This youth knew not what he did. The fault was mine for exposing myself thus hastily. As you value the goodwill in which I hold you all, keep this matter to yourselves. We are not prince or subject today, but comrades bent on sport together. Remember and obey my behest. It is not often I lay my commands upon you."

These words were listened to with gratitude and relief by all the party save one, and his brow gloomed darker than before. Arthyn saw it, and sprang towards Alphonso, who was smiling at his sister in response to her quick words of praise.

"It was his fault—his," she cried, pointing to the scowling Raoul, who looked ill-pleased at having his lips thus sealed. "He insulted him—he insulted me. No man worthy the name would stand still and listen. It is the way with these fine gallants of England. They are ever stirring up strife, and my countrymen bear the blame, the punishment, the odium—"

But Alphonso took her hand with a gesture of boyish chivalry.

"None shall injure thee or thine whilst I am by, sweet Arthyn. The nation is dear to me for thy sake, and thy countrymen shall be as our honoured guests and brothers. Have we not learned to love them for thy sake and their own? Trouble not thy head more over this mischance, and let it not cloud our day's sport.

"Raoul," he added, with some sternness, "thou art a turbulent spirit, and thou lackest the gentle courtesy of a true knight towards those whose position is trying and difficult. Thou wilt not win thy spurs if thou mendest not thy ways. Give thy hand now, before my eyes, to the youth thou didst provoke. If thou marrest the day's pleasure again, I shall have more to say to thee yet."

It was not often that the gentle Alphonso spoke in such tones, and therefore his words were the more heeded. Raoul, inwardly consumed with rage at being thus singled out for rebuke, dared not withstand the order given him, and grudgingly held out his hand. It was not with much greater alacrity that Llewelyn took it, for there was much stubborn sullenness in his disposition, and his passion, though quickly aroused, did not quickly abate; but there was a compulsion in the glance of the royal boy which enforced obedience; and harmony being thus nominally restored, the party once more breathed freely.

"And now upwards and onwards for the lair of the wolf," cried Alphonso; "we have lost time enough already. Who knows the way to his favourite haunts? Methinks they cannot be very far away now."

"I should have thought we had had enough of Welsh wolves for one day," muttered Raoul sullenly to Godfrey; but the latter gave him a warning glance, and he forbore to speak more on the subject.

Gertrude had watched the whole scene with dilated eyes, and a feeling of sympathy and repulsion she was perfectly unable to analyze. When the party moved on again she stole up to

Wendot's side, and said as she glanced into his troubled face:

"He did not mean it? he will not do it again?"

Wendot glanced down at her with a start, and shook his head.

"He knew not that it was the king's son—that I verily believe; but I know not what Llewelyn may say or do at any time. He never speaks to me of what is in his head. Lady Gertrude, you know the king and his ways. Will he visit this rash deed upon my brother's head? Will Llewelyn suffer for what he did in an impulse of mad rage, provoked to it by yon haughty youth, whose words and bearing are hard for any of us to brook?"

"Not if Alphonso can but get his ear; not if this thing is kept secret, as he desires, as he has commanded. But I fear what Raoul may say and do. He is treacherous, selfish, designing. The king thinks well of him, but we love him not. I trust all will yet be well."

"But you fear it may not," added Wendot, completing the sentence as she had not the heart to do. "I fear the same thing myself. But tell me again, Lady Gertrude, what would be the penalty of such an act? Will they—"

"Alphonso has great influence with his father," answered Gertrude quickly. "He will stand your brother's friend through all; perchance he may be detained in some sort of captivity; perchance he may not have his lands restored if this thing comes to the king's ears. But his person will be safe. Fear not for that. Methinks Alphonso would sooner lay down his own life than that harm should befall from what chanced upon a day of sport planned by him and Joanna."

And Gertrude, seeing that a load lay upon the heart of the

Evelyn Everett-Green

young Lord of Dynevor, set herself to chase the cloud from his brow, and had so far succeeded that he looked himself again by the time a warning shout from those in advance showed that some tracks of the wild creature of whom they were in pursuit had been discovered in the path.

"Do not run into danger," pleaded Gertrude, laying a hand on Wendot's arm as he moved quickly forward to the front. "You are so brave you never think of yourself; but do not let us have more bloodshed today, save the blood of the ravenous beast if it must be. I could find it in my heart to wish that we had not come forth on this errand. The brightness of the day has been clouded over."

Wendot answered by a responsive glance. There was something soothing to him in the unsolicited sympathy of Gertrude. He had thought little since they parted two years before of that childish pledge given and received, although he always wore her talisman about his neck, and sometimes looked at it with a smile. He had no serious thoughts of trying to mate with an English noble's daughter. He had had no leisure to spare for thoughts of wedlock at all. But something in the trustful glance of those dark eyes looking confidingly up to him sent a quick thrill through his pulses, which was perhaps the first dawning life of the love of a brave heart.

But there was an impatient call from the front, and Wendot sprang forward, the huntsman awakening within him at the sight of the slot of the quarry. He looked intently at the tracks in the soft earth, and then pointed downwards in the direction of a deep gully or cavernous opening in the hillside, which looked very dark and gloomy to the party who stood in the sunshine of the open.

"The beast has gone that way," he said; "and by his tracks

and these bloodstains, he has prey in his mouth. Likely his mate may have her lair in yon dark spot, and they may be rearing their young in that safe retreat. See how the dogs strain and pant! They smell the prey, and are eager to be off. We must be alert and wary, for wolves with young ones to guard are fierce beyond their wont."

He looked doubtfully at the girls, whose faces were full of mingled terror and excitement. Godfrey read his meaning, and suggested that the ladies should remain in this vantage ground whilst some of the rest went forward to reconnoitre.

But Joanna, ever bold and impetuous, would have none of that.

"We will go on together," she said. "We shall be safest so. No wolf, however fierce, will attack a number like ourselves. They will fly if they can, and if they are brought to bay we need not go near them. But why have we come so far to give up all the peril and the sport at the last moment?"

"She speaks truth," said Wendot, to whom she seemed to look. "At this season of the year wolves have meat in plenty, and will not attack man save in self defence. If we track them silently to their lair, we may surprise and kill the brood; but we are many, and can leave force enough to defend the ladies whilst the rest fight the battle with the creatures at bay."

Nobody really wished to be left behind, and there was a pleasant feeling of safety in numbers. Slowly and cautiously they all followed the track of the wolf downwards into the gloomy ravine, which seemed to shut out all light of the sun between walls of solid rock.

It was a curious freak in which nature had indulged in the formation of this miniature crevasse between the hillsides. At

Evelyn Everett-Green

the base ran a dark turbid stream, which had hollowed out for itself a sort of cavernous opening, and the walls of rock rose almost precipitately on three sides, only leaving one track by which the ravine could be entered. The stream came bubbling out from the rock, passing through some underground passage; and within the gloomy cavern thus produced the savage beasts had plainly made their lair, for there were traces of blood and bones upon the little rocky platform, and the trained ear of Wendot, who was foremost, detected the sound of subdued and angry growling proceeding from the natural cave they were approaching.

"The beasts are in there," he said, pausing, and the next moment Raoul had loosed the dogs, who darted like arrows from bows along the narrow track; and immediately a great he wolf had sprung out with a cry of almost human rage, and had fastened upon one of the assailants, whose piercing yell made the girls shrink back and almost wish they had not come.

But Wendot was not far behind. He was not one of the huntsmen who give all the peril to the dogs and keep out of the fray themselves. Drawing his long hunting knife, and shouting to his brothers to follow him, he sprang down upon the rocky platform himself, and Llewelyn and Howel were at his side in a moment. Godfrey would fain have followed, but his duty obliged him to remain by the side of the princess; and he kept a firm though respectful grasp upon Alphonso's arm, feeling that he must not by any means permit the heir of England to adventure himself into the fray. And indeed the boy's gashed hand hindered him from the use of his weapon, and he could only look on with the most intense interest whilst the conflict between the two fierce beasts and their angry cubs was waged by the fearless lads, who had been through many such encounters before, and showed such skill, such address, such intrepidity in their attack, that the young prince shouted aloud in admiration, and even the girls lost their first sense of terror in the certainty of victory on the side of the Welsh youths.

As for Raoul Latimer, he stood at a safe distance cheering on his dogs, but not adventuring himself within reach of the murderous fangs of the wolves. He occupied a position halfway between the spot upon which the fray was taking place and the vantage ground occupied by the royal party in full sight of the strife.

Arthyn had passed several scornful comments upon the care the young gallant was taking of himself, when suddenly there was a cry from the spectators; for one of the cubs, escaping from the melee, ran full tilt towards Raoul, blind as it seemed with terror; and as it came within reach of his weapon, the sharp blade gleamed in the air, and the little creature gave one yell and rolled over in its death agony. But that cry seemed to pierce the heart of the mother wolf, and suddenly, with almost preternatural strength and activity, she bounded clean over the forms of men and dogs, and dashed straight at Raoul with all the ferocity of an animal at bay, and of a mother robbed of her young.

The young man saw the attack; but his weapon was buried in the body of the cub, and he had no time to disengage it. Turning with a sharp cry of terror, he attempted to fly up the rocky path; but the beast was upon him. She made a wild dash and fastened upon his back, her fangs crushing one shoulder and her hot breath seeming to scorch his cheek. With a wild yell of agony and terror Raoul threw himself face downwards upon the ground, whilst his cry was shrilly echoed by the girls—all but Arthyn, who stood rigidly as if turned to stone, a strange, fierce light blazing in her eyes.

But help was close at hand. Wendot had seen the spring, and

had followed close upon the charge of the maddened brute. Flinging himself fearlessly upon the struggling pair, he plunged his knife into the neck of the wolf, causing her to relax her hold of her first foe and turn upon him. Had he stabbed her to the heart she might have inflicted worse injury upon Raoul in her mortal struggle; as it was, there was fierce fight left in her still. But Wendot was kneeling upon the wildly struggling body with all his strength, and had locked his hands fast round her throat.

"Quick, Llewelyn—the knife!" he cried, and his brother was beside him in an instant.

The merciful death stroke was given, and the three youths rose from their crouching posture and looked each other in the eyes, whilst the wolf lay still and dead by the side of her cub.

"Methinks we have had something too much of Welsh wolves," was the only comment of Raoul, as he joined the royal party without a word to the brothers who had saved his life.

CHAPTER VII

THE KING'S JUDGMENT

The great King Edward had been sitting enthroned in the state apartment of the castle, receiving the homage of those amongst the Welsh lords and chieftains who had been summoned to pay their homage to him and had obeyed this summons.

It was an imposing sight, and one not likely to be forgotten by any who witnessed it for the first time. The courageous but gentle Queen Eleanor, who was seldom absent from her lord's side be the times peaceful or warlike, was seated beside him for the ceremony, with her two elder daughters beside her. The young Alphonso stood at the right hand of the king, his face bright with interest and sympathy; and if ever the act of homage seemed to be paid with effort by some rugged chieftain, or he saw a look of gloom or pain upon the face of such a one, he was ever ready with some graceful speech or small act of courtesy, which generally acted like a charm. And the father regarded his son with a fond pride, and let him take his own way with these haughty, untamable spirits, feeling perhaps that the tact of the royal boy would do more to conciliate and win hearts than any word or deed of his own.

Evelyn Everett-Green

Edward has been often harshly condemned for his cruelty and treachery towards the vanquished Welsh; but it must be remembered with regard to the first charge that the days were rude and cruel, that the spirit of the age was fierce and headstrong, and that the barons and nobles who were scheming for the fair lands of Wales were guilty of many of the unjust and oppressive acts for which Edward has since been held responsible. The Welsh were themselves a very wild race, in some parts of the country barely civilized; and there can be no denying that a vein of fierce treachery ran through their composition, and that they often provoked their adversaries to cruel retaliation. As for the king himself, his policy was on the whole a merciful and just one, if the one point of his feudal supremacy were conceded. To those who came to him with their act of homage he confirmed their possession of ancestral estates, and treated them with kindness and consideration. He was too keen a statesman and too just a man to desire anything but a conciliatory policy so far as it was possible. Only when really roused to anger and resolved upon war did the fiercer side of his nature show itself, and then, indeed, he could show himself terrible and lion-like in his wrath.

The brothers of Dynevor were the last of those who came to pay their act of homage. The day had waned, and the last light of sunset was streaming into that long room as the fair-haired Wendot bent his knee in response to the summons of the herald. The king's eyes seemed to rest upon him with interest, and he spoke kindly to the youth; but it was noted by some in the company that his brow darkened when Llewelyn followed his brother's example, Howel attending him as Griffeth had supported Wendot; and there was none of the gracious urbanity in the royal countenance now that had characterized it during the past hour.

Several faces amongst those in immediate attendance upon

the king and his family watched this closing scene with unwonted interest. Gertrude stood with Joanna's hand clasped in hers, quivering with excitement, and ever and anon casting quick looks towards her brother, who stood behind the chair of state observant and watchful, but without betraying his feelings either by word or look. Raoul Latimer was there, a sneer upon his lips, a malevolent light in his eyes, which deepened as they rested upon Llewelyn, whilst Arthyn watched the twin brothers with a strange look in her glowing eyes, her lips parted, her white teeth just showing between, her whole expression one of tense expectancy and sympathy. Once Llewelyn glanced up and met the look she bent on him. A dusky flush overspread his cheek, and his fingers clenched themselves in an unconscious movement understood only by himself.

The homage paid, there was a little stir at the lower end of the hall as the doors were flung open for the royal party to take their departure. Edward bent a searching look upon the four brothers, who had fallen back somewhat, and were clustered together not far from the royal group, and the next minute an attendant whispered to them that it was the king's pleasure they should follow in his personal retinue, as he had somewhat to say to them in private.

Wendot's heart beat rather faster than its wont. He had had some foreboding of evil ever since that unlucky expedition, some days back now, on which Llewelyn's sword had been drawn upon an English subject, and had injured the king's son likewise. Raoul had for very shame affected a sort of condescending friendliness towards the brothers after they had been instrumental in saving him from the fangs of the she wolf; but it was pretty evident to them that his friendship was but skin deep; whilst every word that passed between Arthyn and Llewelyn or his brother—and these were many—was ranked as a dire offence.

Had Wendot been more conversant with the intrigues of courts, he would have seen plainly that Raoul was paying his addresses to the Welsh heiress, who plainly detested and abhorred him. The ambitious and clever young man, who was well thought of by the king, and had many friends amongst the nobles and barons, had a plan of his own for securing to himself some of the richest territory in the country, and was leaving no stone unturned in order to achieve that object. A marriage with Arthyn would give him the hold he wanted upon a very large estate. But indifferent as he was to the feelings of the lady, he was wise enough to see that whilst she remained in her present mood, and was the confidante and friend of the princesses, he should not gain the king's consent to prosecuting his nuptials by force, as he would gladly have done. Whereupon a new scheme had entered his busy brain, as a second string to his bow, and with the help of a kinsman high in favour with the king, he had great hopes of gaining his point, which would at once gratify his ambition and inflict vengeance upon a hated rival.

Raoul had hated the Dynevor brothers ever since he had detected in Arthyn an interest in and sympathy for them, ever since he had found her in close talk in their own tongue with the dark-browed twins, whose antagonism to the English was scarcely disguised. He had done all he knew to stir the hot blood in Llewelyn and Howel, and that with some success. The lads were looked upon as dangerous and treacherous by many of those in the castle; and from the sneering look of coming triumph upon the face of young Latimer as the party moved off towards the private apartments of the royal family, it was plain that he anticipated a victory for himself and a profound humiliation for his foes.

Supper was the first business of the hour, and the Dynevor brothers sat at the lower table with the attendants of the king. The meal was well-served and plentiful, but they bad small appetite for it. Wendot felt as though a shadow hung upon them; and the chief comfort he received was in stealing glances at the sweet, sensitive face of Gertrude, who generally responded to his glance by one of her flashing smiles.

Wendot wondered how it was that Lord Montacute had never sought him out to speak to him. Little as the lad had thought of their parting interview at Dynevor during the past two years, it all came back with the greatest vividness as he looked upon the fine calm face of the English noble. Was it possible he had forgotten the half-pledge once given him? Or did he regret it, now that his daughter was shooting up from a child into a sweet and gracious maiden whom he felt disposed to worship with reverential awe? Wendot did not think he was in love—he would scarce have known the meaning of the phrase and he as little understood the feelings which had lately awakened within him; but he did feel conscious that a new element had entered into his life, and with it a far less bitter sense of antagonism to the English than he had experienced in previous years.

After the supper was ended the royal family withdrew into an inner room, and presently the four brothers were bidden to enter, as the king had somewhat to say to them. The greater number of the courtiers and attendants remained in the outer room, but Sir Godfrey Challoner, Raoul Latimer, and one or two other gentlemen were present in the smaller apartment. The queen and royal children were also there, and their playfellows and companions, Gertrude holding her father by the hand, and watching with intense interest the approach of the brothers and the faces of the king and his son.

Edward was seated before a table on which certain parchments lay. Alphonso stood beside him, and Wendot fancied that he had only just ended some earnest appeal, his parted lips and flushed cheeks seeming to tell of recent eager speech. The king looked keenly at the brothers as they made their obeisance to him, and singling out Wendot, bid him by a gesture to approach nearer.

There was a kindliness in the royal countenance which encouraged the youth, and few could approach the great soldier king without experiencing something of the fascination which his powerful individuality exercised over all his subjects.

"Come hither, boy," he said; "we have heard nought but good of thee. Thou hast an eloquent advocate in yon maiden of Lord Montacute's, and mine own son and daughters praise thy gallantry in no measured terms. We have made careful examination into these parchments here, containing reports of the late rebellion, and cannot find that thou hast had part or lot in it. Thou hast paid thy homage without dallying or delay; wherefore it is our pleasure to confirm to thee thy possession of thy castle of Dynevor and its territory. We only caution thee to remain loyal to him thou hast owned as king, and we will establish thee in thy rights if in time to come they be disputed by others, or thou stirrest up foes by thy loyalty to us."

Wendot bowed low. If there was something bitter in having his father's rightful inheritance granted to him as something of a boon, at least there was much to sweeten the draught in the kindly and gracious bearing of the king, and in Alphonso's friendly words and looks. He had no father to look to in time of need, and felt a great distrust of the kinsman who exercised some guardianship over him; so that there was considerable relief for the youth in feeling that the great King of England was his friend, and that he would keep him from the aggression of foes.

He stood aside as Edward's glance passed on to Llewelyn

and Howel, and it was plain that the monarch's face changed and hardened as he fixed his eye upon the twins.

"Llewelyn—Howel," he said, "joint lords of Iscennen, we wish that we had received the same good report of you that we have done of your brethren. But it is not so. There be dark records in your past which give little hope for the future. Nevertheless you are yet young. Wisdom may come with the advance of years. But the hot blood in you requires taming and curbing. You have proved yourselves unfit for the place hitherto occupied as lords of the broad lands bequeathed you by Res Vychan, your father. For the present those lands are forfeit. You must win the right to call them yours again by loyalty in the cause which every true Welshman should have at heart, because it is the cause which alone can bring peace and safety to your harassed country. It is not willingly that we wrest from any man the lands that are his birthright. Less willingly do we do this when homage, however unwilling and reluctant, has been paid. But we have our duties to ourselves and to our submitted subjects to consider, and it is not meet to send firebrands alight into the world, when a spark may raise so fierce a conflagration, and when hundreds of lives have to pay the penalty of one mad act of headstrong youth. It is your youth that shall be your excuse from the charge of graver offence, but those who are too young to govern themselves are not fit to govern others."

Whilst the king had been speaking he had been closely studying the faces of the twin brothers, who stood before him with their eyes on the ground. These two lads, although by their stature and appearance almost men, had not attained more than their sixteenth year, and had by no means learned that control of feature which is one of nature's hardest lessons. As the king's words made themselves understood, their brows had darkened and their faces had contracted with a fierce anger and rage, which betrayed itself also in their

Evelyn Everett-Green

clenched hands and heaving chests; and although they remained speechless—for the awe inspired by Edward's presence could not but make itself felt even by them—it was plain that only the strongest efforts put upon themselves hindered them from some outbreak of great violence.

Edward's eye rested sternly upon them for a moment, and then he addressed himself once again to Wendot.

"To thee, Res Wendot," he said, "we give the charge of these two turbulent brothers of thine. Had not the Prince Alphonso spoken for them, we had kept them under our own care here in our fortress of Rhuddlan. But he has pleaded for them that they have their liberty, therefore into thy charge do we give them. Take them back with thee to Dynevor, and strive to make them like unto thyself and thy shadow there, who is, they tell me, thy youngest brother, and as well disposed as thyself.

"Say, young man, wilt thou accept this charge, and be surety for these haughty youths? If their own next-of-kin will not take this office, we must look elsewhere for a sterner guardian."

For a moment Wendot hesitated, He knew well the untamable spirit of his brothers, and the small influence he was likely to have upon them, and for a moment his heart shrank from the task. But again he bethought what his refusal must mean to them—captivity of a more or less irksome kind, harsh treatment perhaps, resulting in actual imprisonment, and a sure loss of favour with any guardian who had the least love for the English cause. At Dynevor they would at least be free.

Surely, knowing all, they would not make his task too hard. The tie of kindred was very close. Wendot remembered words spoken by the dying bed of his parents, and his mind was quickly made up.

"I will be surety for them," he said briefly. "If they offend again, let my life, my lands, be the forfeit."

The monarch gave him a searching glance. Perhaps some of the effort with which he had spoken made itself audible in his tones. He looked full at Wendot for a brief minute, and then turned to the black-browed twins.

"You hear your brother's pledge," he said in low, stern tones. "If you have the feelings of men of honour, you will respect the motive which prompts him to give it, and add no difficulties to the task he has imposed upon himself. Be loyal to him, and loyal to the cause he has embraced, and perchance a day may come when you may so have redeemed your past youthful follies as to claim and receive at our hands the lands we now withhold. In the meantime they will be administered by Raoul Latimer, who will draw the revenues and maintain order there. He has proved his loyalty in many ways ere this, and he is to be trusted, as one day I hope you twain may be."

Llewelyn started as if he had been stung as these words crossed the king's lips. His black eyes flashed fire, and as he lifted his head and met the mocking glance of Raoul, it seemed for a moment as if actually in the presence of the king he would have flown at his antagonist's throat; but Wendot's hand was on his arm, and even Howel had the self-command to whisper a word of caution. Alphonso sprang gaily between the angry youth and his father's keen glance, and began talking eagerly of Dynevor, asking how the brothers would spend their time, now that they were all to live there once more; whilst Arthyn, coming forward, drew Llewelyn gently backward, casting at Raoul a look of such bitter scorn and hatred that he involuntarily shrank before it.

"Thou hast taken a heavy burden upon thy young shoulders, lad," said a well-remembered voice in Wendot's ear, and looking up, he met the calm gaze of Lord Montacute bent upon him; whilst Gertrude, flushing and sparkling, stood close beside her father. "Thinkest thou that such tempers as those will be easily controlled?"

Wendot's face was grave, and looked manly in its noble thoughtfulness.

"I know not what to say; but, in truth, I could have given no other answer. Could I leave my own brethren to languish in captivity, however honourable, when a word from me would free them? Methinks, sir, thou scarce knowest what freedom is to us wild sons of Wales, or how the very thought of any hindrance to perfect liberty chafes our spirit and frets us past the limit of endurance. Sooner than be fettered by bonds, however slack, I would spring from yonder casement and dash myself to pieces upon the stones below. To give my brothers up into unfriendly hands would be giving them up to certain death. If my spirit could not brook such control, how much less could theirs?"

Gertrude's soft eyes gave eloquent and sympathetic response. Wendot had unconsciously addressed his justification to her rather than to her father. Her quick sympathy gave him heart and hope. She laid her hand upon his arm and said:

"I think thou art very noble, Wendot; it was like thee to do it. I was almost grieved when I heard thee take the charge upon thyself, for I fear it may be one of peril to thee. But I love thee the more for thy generosity. Thou wilt be a true and brave knight ere thou winnest thy spurs in battle."

Wendot's face flushed with shy happiness at hearing such frank and unqualified praise from one he was beginning to hold so dear. Lord Montacute laid his hand smilingly on his daughter's mouth, as if to check her ready speech, and then bidding her join the Lady Joanna, who was making signals to her from the other side of the room, he drew Wendot a little away into an embrasure, and spoke to him in tones of considerable gravity.

"Young man," he said, "I know not if thou hast any memory left of the words I spake to thee when last we met at Dynevor?"

Wendot's colour again rose, but his glance did not waver.

"I remember right well," he answered simply. "I spoke words then of which I have often thought since—words that I have not repented till today, nor indeed till I heard thee pass that pledge which makes thee surety for thy turbulent brothers."

A quick, troubled look crossed Wendot's face, but he did not speak, and Lord Montacute continued—"I greatly fear that thou hast undertaken more than thou canst accomplish; and that, instead of drawing thy brothers from the paths of peril, thou wilt rather be led by them into treacherous waters, which may at last overwhelm thee. You are all young together, and many dangers beset the steps of youth. Thou art true and loyal hearted, that I know well; but thou art a Welshman, and—"

He paused and stopped short, and Wendot answered, not without pride:

"I truly am a Welshman—it is my boast to call myself that. If you fear to give your daughter to one of that despised race, so be it. I would not drag her down to degradation; I love her

Evelyn Everett-Green

too well for that. Keep her to thyself. I give thee back thy pledge."

Lord Montacute smiled as he laid his hand upon the young man's shoulder.

"So hot and hasty, Wendot, as hasty as those black-haired twins. Yet, boy, I like thee for thy outspoken candour, and I would not have thee change it for the smooth treachery of courtly intrigue. If I had nought else to think of, I would plight my daughter's hand to thee, an ye both were willing, more gladly than to any man I know. But, Wendot, she is mine only child, and very dear to me. There are others who would fain win her smiles, others who would be proud to do her lightest behest. She is yet but a child. Perchance she has not seriously considered these matters. Still there will come a time when she will do so, and—"

"Then let her choose where she will," cried Wendot, proudly and hotly. "Think you I would wed one whose heart was given elsewhere? Take back your pledge—think of it no more. If the day comes when I may come to her free and unfettered, and see if she has any regard for me, good. I will come. But so long as you hold that peril menaces my path, I will not ask her even to think of me. Let her forget. I will not bind her by a word. It shall be as if those words had never passed betwixt us."

Lord Montacute scarce knew if regret, relief, or admiration were the feeling uppermost in his mind, as the youth he believed so worthy of his fair daughter, and perhaps not entirely indifferent to her dawning charms, thus frankly withdrew his claim upon her hand. It seems strange to us that any one should be talking and thinking so seriously of matrimony when the girl was but fourteen and the youth three years her senior; but in those days marriages were not only planned but consummated at an absurdly early age according to our modern notions, and brides of fifteen and sixteen were considered almost mature. Many young men of Wendot's age would be seriously seeking a wife, and although no such thought had entered his head until he had seen Gertrude again, it cannot be denied that the idea had taken some hold upon him now, or that he did not feel a qualm of pain and sorrow at thus yielding up one bright hope just when the task he had taken upon himself seemed to be clouding his life with anxiety and peril.

"Boy," said Lord Montacute, "I cannot forget what thou hast done nor what she owes to thee. I love thee well, and would fain welcome thee as a son; but my love for her bids me wait till we see what is the result of this office thou hast taken on thyself. Thou hast acted rightly and nobly, but in this world trouble often seems to follow the steps of those who strive most after the right. If thine own life, thine own possessions, are to pay the forfeit if thy brethren fall away into rebellion—and Edward, though a just man and kind, can be stern to exact the uttermost penalty when he is angered or defied—then standest thou in sore peril, peril from which I would shield my maid. Wherefore—"

"Nay, say no more—say no more. I comprehend it all too well," replied Wendot, not without a natural though only momentary feeling of bitterness at the thought of what this pledge was already costing him, but his native generosity and sweetness of temper soon triumphed over all besides, and he said with his peculiarly bright and steadfast smile, "You have judged rightly and well for us both, my lord. Did I but drag her down to sorrow and shame, it would be the bitterest drop in a bitter cup. A man placed as I am is better without ties."

"Also the days will soon pass by, and the time will come

Evelyn Everett-Green

when this charge ceases. Then if the Lady Gertrude be still mistress of her hand and heart, and if the Lord of Dynevor comes to try his fate, methinks, by what I have seen and heard, that he may chance to get no unkindly answer to his wooing."

Wendot made no reply, but only blushed deeply as he moved away. He scarce knew whether he were glad or sorry that Gertrude came out to meet him, and drew him towards the little group which had gathered in a deep embrasure of the window. Joanna, Alphonso, and Griffeth were there. They had been eagerly questioning the younger lad about life at Dynevor, and what they would do when they were at home all together. Joanna was longing to travel that way and lodge a night there; and Gertrude was eloquent in praise of the castle, and looked almost wistfully at Wendot to induce him to add his voice to the general testimony. But he was unwontedly grave and silent, and her soft eyes filled with tears. She knew that he was heavy hearted, and it cut her to the quick; but he did not speak of his trouble, and only Alphonso ventured to allude to it, and that was by one quick sentence as he was taking his departure at bedtime.

"Wendot," he said earnestly, "I will ever be thy friend. Fear not. My father denies me nothing. Thy trial may be a hard one, but thou wilt come nobly forth from it. I will see that harm to thee comes not from thy generosity. Only be true to us, and thou shalt not suffer."

Wendot made no reply, but the words were like a gleam of sunshine breaking through the clouds; and one more such gleam was in store for him on the morrow, when he bid a final adieu to Gertrude before the general departure for Dynevor.

"I have my half gold coin, Wendot. I shall look at it every

day and think of thee. I am so happy that we have seen each other once again. Thou wilt not forget me, Wendot?"

"Never so long as I live," he answered with sudden fervour, raising the small hand he held to his lips. "And some day, perchance, Lady Gertrude, I will come to thee again."

"I shall be waiting for thee," she answered, with a mixture of arch sweetness and playfulness that he scarce knew whether to call childlike confidence or maiden trust. But the look in her eyes went to his heart, and was treasured there, like the memory of a sunbeam, for many long days to come.

Evelyn Everett-Green

CHAPTER VIII

TURBULENT SPIRITS

The four sons of Res Vychan went back to Dynevor together, there to settle down, outwardly at least, to a quiet and uneventful life, chiefly diversified by hunting and fishing, and such adventures as are inseparable from those pastimes in which eager lads are engrossed.

Wendot both looked and felt older for his experiences in the castle of Rhuddlan. His face had lost much of its boyishness, and had taken a thoughtfulness beyond his years. Sometimes he appeared considerably oppressed by the weight of the responsibility with which he had charged himself, and would watch the movements and listen to the talk of the twins with but slightly concealed uneasiness.

Yet as days merged into weeks, and weeks lengthened into months, and still there had been nothing to alarm him unduly, he began, as the inclement winter drew on, to breathe more freely; for in the winter months all hostilities of necessity ceased, for the mountain passes were always blocked with snow, and both travelling and fighting were practically out of the question for a considerable time.

Wendot, too, had matters enough to occupy his mind quite

apart from the charge of his two haughty brothers. He had his own estates to administer—no light task for a youth not yet eighteen—and his large household to order; and though Griffeth gave him every help, Llewelyn and Howel stood sullenly aloof, and would not appear to take the least interest in anything that appertained to Dynevor, although they gave no reason for their conduct, and were not in other ways unfriendly to their brothers.

The country was for the time being quiet and at peace. Exhausted by its own internal struggles and by the late disastrous campaign against the English, the land was, as it were, resting and recruiting itself, in preparation, perhaps, for another outbreak later on. In the meantime, sanguine spirits like those of Wendot and Griffeth began to cherish hopes that the long and weary struggle was over at last, and that the nation, as a nation, would begin to realize the wisdom and the advantage of making a friend and ally of the powerful monarch of England, instead of provoking him to acts of tyranny and retaliation by perpetual and fruitless rebellions against a will far too strong to be successfully resisted.

But Llewelyn and Howel never spoke of the English without words and looks indicative of the deepest hatred; and the smouldering fire in their breasts was kept glowing and burning by the wild words and the wilder songs of the old bard Wenwynwyn, who spent the best part of his time shut up in his own bare room, with his harp for his companion, in which room Llewelyn and Howel spent much of their time during the dark winter days, when they could be less and less out of doors.

Since that adventure of the Eagle's Crag, Wendot had distrusted the old minstrel, and was uneasy at the influence he exercised upon the twins; but the idea of sending him from Dynevor was one which never for a moment entered his head. Had not Wenwynwyn grown old in his father's service? Had he not been born and bred at Dynevor? The young lord himself seemed to have a scarce more assured right to his place there than the ancient bard. Be he friend or be he foe, at Dynevor he must remain so long as the breath remained in his body.

The bard was, by hereditary instinct, attached to all the boys, but of late there had been but little community of thought between him and his young chieftain. Wendot well knew the reason. The old man hated the English with the bitter, unreasoning, deadly hatred of his wild, untutored nature. Had he not sprung from a race whose lives had been spent in rousing in the breasts of all who heard them the most fervent and unbounded patriotic enthusiasm? And was it to be marvelled at that he could not see or understand the changes of the times or the hopelessness of the long struggle, now that half the Welsh nobles were growing cool in the national cause, and the civilization and wealth of the sister country were beginning to show them that their own condition left much to be desired, and that there was something better and higher to be achieved than a so-called liberty, only maintained at the cost of perpetual bloodshed? or a series of petty feuds for supremacy, which went far to keep the land in a state of semi-barbarism?

So the old bard sang his wild songs, and Llewelyn and Howel sat by the glowing fire of logs that blazed in the long winter evenings upon his hearth, listening to his fierce words, and hardening their hearts and bracing their wills against any kind of submission to a foreign yoke. A burning hatred against the English king also consumed them. Had they not, at the cost of most bitter humiliation, gone to him as vassals, trusting to his promise that all who did homage for their lands should be confirmed in peaceful possession of the same? And how had he treated this act of painful submission? Was it greatly to be wondered at that their hearts burned with an unquenchable hatred? To them Edward stood as the type of all that was cruel and treacherous and grasping. They brooded over their wrongs by day and by night; they carried their dark looks with them when they stirred abroad or when they rested at home. Wenwynwyn sympathized as none besides seemed to do, and he became their great solace and chief counsellor.

Wendot might uneasily wonder what passed in that quiet room of the old man's, but he never knew or guessed. He would better have liked to hear Llewelyn burst forth into the old passionate invective. He was uneasy at this chronic state of gloom and sullen silence on the vexed question of English supremacy. But seldom a word passed the lips of either twin. They kept their secret—if secret they had—locked away in their own breasts. And days and weeks and months passed by, and Wendot and Griffeth seemed almost as much alone at Dynevor as they had been after their father's death, when Llewelyn and Howel had betaken themselves to their castle of Carregcennen.

But at least, if silent and sullen, they did not appear to entertain any plan likely to raise anxiety in Wendot's mind as to the pledge he had given to the king. They kept at home, and never spoke of Iscennen, and as the winter passed away and the spring began to awaken the world from her long white sleep, they betook themselves with zest to their pastime of hunting, and went long expeditions that sometimes lasted many days, returning laden with spoil, and apparently in better spirits from the bracing nature of their pursuits.

Griffeth, who had felt the cold somewhat keenly, and had been drooping and languid all the winter, picked up strength and spirit as the days grew longer and warmer, and began to

Evelyn Everett-Green

enjoy open-air life once more.

Wendot was much wrapped up in this young brother of his, who had always been dearer to him than any being in the world besides.

Since he had been at death's door with the fever, Griffeth had never recovered the robustness of health which had hitherto been the characteristic of the Dynevor brothers all their lives. He was active and energetic when the fit was on him, but he wearied soon of any active sport. He could no longer bound up the mountain paths with the fleetness and elasticity of a mountain deer, and in the keen air of the higher peaks it was difficult for him to breathe.

Still in the summer days he was almost his former self again, or so Wendot hoped; and although Griffeth's lack of rude health hindered both from joining the long expeditions planned and carried out by the twins, it never occurred to Wendot to suspect that there was an ulterior motive for these, or to realize how unwelcome his presence would have been had he volunteered it, in lieu of staying behind with Griffeth, and contenting himself with less adventurous sports.

Spring turned to summer, and summer to autumn, and life at Dynevor seemed to move quietly enough. Griffeth took a fancy to book learning—a rare enough accomplishment in those days—and a monk from the Abbey of Strata Florida was procured to give him instruction in the obscure science of reading and writing. Wendot, who had a natural love of study, and who had been taught something of these mysteries by his mother—she being for the age she lived in a very cultivated woman—shared his brother's studies, and delighted in the acquirement of learning.

But this new development on the part of the Lord of Dynevor

and his brother seemed to divide them still more from the two remaining sons of Res Vychan; and the old bard would solemnly shake his head and predict certain ruin to the house when its master laid aside sword for pen, and looked for counsel to the monk and missal instead of to his good right hand and his faithful band of armed retainers.

Wendot and Griffeth would smile at these dark sayings, and loved their studies none the less because they opened out before them some better understanding of the blessings of peace and culture upon a world harried and exhausted with perpetual, aimless strife; but their more enlightened opinions seemed but to widen the breach between them and their brothers, and soon they began to be almost strangers to each other.

Wendot and Griffeth regretted this without seeing how to mend matters. They felt sorry for Llewelyn and Howel, deprived of the employments and authority they had enjoyed of late, and would have gladly given them a share of authority in Dynevor; but this they would not accept, drawing more and more away into themselves, and sharing their confidences with no one except Wenwynwyn.

The summer was now on the wane, and the blustering winds of the equinox had begun to moan about the castle walls. The men were busy getting in the last of the fruits of the earth and storing them up against the winter need, whilst the huntsmen brought in day by day stores of venison and game, which the women salted down for consumption during the long dreary days when snow should shut them within their own walls, and no fresh meat would be obtainable.

It was a busy season, and Wendot had time and mind alike full. He heeded little the movements of his brothers, whom he thought engrossed in the pleasures of the chase. He was not even aware that old Wenwynwyn was absent for several days from the castle, for since the estrangement between him and the old man he was often days at a time without encountering him.

Llewelyn and Howel were visibly restless just now. They did not go far from the castle, nor did they seem interested in the spoil the hunters brought home. But they spent many long hours in the great gallery where the arms of the retainers were laid up, and their heads were often to be seen close together in deep discussion, although if any person came near to disturb them they would spring asunder, or begin loudly discussing some indifferent theme.

They were in this vast, gloomy place, sitting together in the deep embrasure of one of the narrow windows as the daylight began to fail, when suddenly they beheld Wenwynwyn stalking through the long gallery as if in search of them, and they sprang forward to greet him with unconcealed eagerness.

"Thou hast returned."

"Ay, my sons, I have returned, and am the bearer of good news. But this is not the place to speak. Stones have ears, and traitors abound even in these hoary walls which have echoed to the songs of the bard for more years than man can count. Ah, woe the day; ah, woe the falling off! That I should live to see the sons of Dynevor thus fall away—the young eaglets leaving their high estate to grovel with the carrion vulture and the coward crow! Ah! in old days it was not so. But there are yet those of the degenerate race in whom the spirit of their fathers burns. Come, my sons—come hither with me. I bring you a message from Iscennen that will gladden your hearts to hear."

The boys pressed after him up the narrow, winding stair that led to the room the bard called his own. It was remote from the rest of the castle, and words spoken within its walls could be heard by none outside. It was a place that had heard much plotting and planning ere now, and what was to be spoken tonight was but the sequel of what had gone before.

"Speak, Wenwynwyn, speak!" cried the twins in a breath. "Has he returned thither?"

"Ay, my sons; he has come back in person to receive his 'dues,' and to look into all that has passed in his absence. These eyes have seen the false, smiling face of the usurper, who sits in the halls which have rung to the sound of yon harp in days when the accursed foot of the stranger would have been driven with blows from the door. He is there, and—"

"And they hate and despise and contemn him," cried Llewelyn in wild excitement. "Every man of Iscennen is his foe. Do not I know it? Have we not proved it? There is no one but will rise at the sound of my trumpet, to follow me to victory or death.

"Wenwynwyn, speak! thou hast bid us wait till the hour has come till all things be ripe for action. Tell us, has not that hour come? Hast thou not come to bid us draw the sword, and wrest our rightful inheritance from the hand of the spoiler and alien?"

"Ay, verily, that hour has come," cried the old bard, with a wild gesture. "The spoiler is there, lurking in his den. His eyes are roving round in hungry greed to spoil the poor man of his goods, to wrest the weapon from the strong. He is fearful in the midst of his state—fearful of those he calls his vassals—those he would crush with his iron glove, and wring dry even as a sponge is wrung. Ay, the hour is come. The loyal patriots have looked upon your faces, my sons, and see in you their liberators. Go now, when the traitor whose life you saved is gloating over his spoil in his castle walls. Go and show him what it is to rob the young lions of their prey; show him what it is to strive with eagles, when only the blood of the painted jay runs in his craven veins. Saw I not fear, distrust, and hatred in every line of that smooth face? Think you that he is happy in the possession of what he sold his soul to gain? Go, and the victory will be yours. Go; all Iscennen will be with you. Wenwynwyn has not sung his songs in vain amongst those hardy people! He has prepared the way. Go! victory lies before you."

The boys' hearts swelled within them at these words. It was not for nothing that they, with their own faithful followers, sworn to secrecy, had absented themselves again and again from Dynevor Castle on the pretence of long hunting expeditions. It was true that they had hunted game, that they had brought home abundance of spoil with them; but little had Llewelyn or Howel to do with the taking of that prey. They had been at Iscennen; they had travelled the familiar tracks once again, and had found nothing but the most enthusiastic welcome from their own people, the greatest hatred for the foreign lordling, who had been foisted upon them by edict of the king.

Truly Raoul Latimer had won but a barren triumph in gaining for himself the lands of Iscennen. A very short residence there had proved enough for him, and he had withdrawn, in fear that if he did not do so some fatal mischance would befall him. He had reigned there as an absentee ever since, not less cursed and hated for the oppressive measures taken in his name than when he had been the active agent.

Matters were ripe for revolt. There only wanted the time and the occasion. The leader was already to hand—the old lord, young in years, Llewelyn ap Res Vychan, and Howel his brother. With the twins at their head, Iscennen would rise to a man; and then let Raoul Latimer look to himself! For the Welsh, when once aroused to strike, struck hard; and it cannot be denied that they ofttimes struck treacherously beside.

Small wonder if, as Wenwynwyn declared, young Raoul had found but small satisfaction in his visit to his new estate, and lived upon it in terror of his very life, though surrounded by the solid walls of his own castle.

The hour had come. Llewelyn and Howel were about to taste the keen joy of revenging themselves upon a foe they hated and abhorred, about to take at least one step towards reinstating themselves in their ancestral halls. But the second object was really less dear to them than the first. If the hated Raoul could be slain, or made to fly in ignominy and disgrace, they cared little who reigned in his place. Their own tenure at Carregcennen under existing circumstances they knew to be most insecure, and although they had organized and were to lead the attack, they were to do so disguised, and those who knew the share they were to take were pledged not to betray it.

Loose as had grown the bond between the brothers of late, the twins were not devoid of a certain rude code of honour of their own, and had no wish to involve Wendot in ruin and disgrace. He was surety for their good behaviour, and if it became known to Edward that they had led the attack on one of his English subjects, Dynevor itself might pay the forfeit of his displeasure, and Wendot might have to answer with his life, as he had offered to do, for his brothers. Thus, though this consideration was not strong enough to keep the twins from indulging their ungovernable hatred to their foe,

Evelyn Everett-Green

it made them cautious about openly appearing in the matter themselves; and when, upon a wild, blustering night not many days later, a little band of hardy Welshmen, all armed to the teeth, crept with the silent caution of wild beasts along a rocky pathway which led by a subterranean way, known only to Llewelyn and Howel, into the keep of the castle itself; none would have recognized in the blackened faces of the two leaders, covered, as they appeared to be, with a tangled growth of hair and beard, the countenances of the sons of Res Vychan; whilst the stalwart, muscular figures seemed rather to belong to men than lads, and assisted the disguise not a little.

The hot-headed but by no means intrepid young Englishman, who had not had the courage to remain long in the possessions he had coveted, and who was fervently wishing that this second visit was safely over, was aroused from his slumbers by the clash of arms, and by the terrified cries of the guard he always placed about him.

"The Welsh wolves are upon us!" he heard a voice cry out in the darkness. "We are undone—betrayed! Every man for himself! They are murdering every soul they meet."

In a passion of rage and terror Raoul sprang from his bed, and commenced hurrying into his clothes as fast as his trembling hands would allow him. In vain he called to his servants; they had every man of them fled. Below he heard the clash of arms, and the terrible guttural cries with which the Welsh always rushed into battle, and which echoed through the halls of Carregcennen like the trump of doom.

It was a terrible moment for the young Englishman, alone, half-armed, and at the mercy of a merciless foe. He looked wildly round for some means of escape. The tread of many feet was on the stairs. To attempt resistance was hopeless.

Flight was the only resource left him, and in a mad impulse of terror he flung himself on the floor, and crept beneath the bed, the arras of which concealed him from sight. There he lay panting and trembling, whilst the door was burst open and armed men came flocking in.

"Ha, flown already!" cried a voice which did not seem entirely unfamiliar to the shivering youth, though he could not have said exactly to whom it belonged, and was in no mood to cudgel his brains on the subject.

He understood too little of the Welsh tongue to follow what was said, but with unspeakable relief he heard steps pass from the room; for even his foes did not credit him with the cowardice which would drive a man to perish like a rat in a hole rather than sword in hand like a knight and a soldier.

The men had dashed out, hot in pursuit, believing him to be attempting escape through some of the many outlets of the castle; and Raoul, still shivering and craven, was just creeping out from his hiding place, resolved to try to find his way to the outer world, when he uttered a gasp and stood or rather crouched spellbound where he was; for, standing beside a table on which the dim light of a night candle burned, binding up a gash in his arm with a scarf belonging to the Englishman, was a tall, stalwart, soldierly figure, that turned quickly at the sound made by the wretched Raoul.

"Spare me, spare me!" cried the miserable youth, as the man with a quick movement grasped his weapon and advanced towards him.

He did not know if his English would be understood, but it appeared to be, for the reply was spoken in the same tongue, though the words had strong Welsh accent.

"And wherefore should I spare you? What have you done that we of Iscennen should look upon you as other than a bitter foe? By what right are you here wringing our life blood from us? Why should I not stamp the miserable life out of you as you lie grovelling at my feet? Wales were well quit of such craven hounds as you."

"Spare me, and I renounce my claim. I swear by all that is holy that if you will but grant me my life I will repair to the king's court without delay, and I will yield up to him every claim which I have on these lands. I swear it by all that is holy in heaven and earth."

"And what good shall we reap from that? We shall but have another English tyrant set over us. Better kill thee outright, as a warning to all who may come after."

But Raoul clasped the knees of his foe, and lifted his voice again in passionate appeal.

"Kill me not; what good would that do you or your cause? I tell you it would but raise Edward's ire, and he would come with fire and sword to devastate these lands as I have never done. Listen, and I will tell you what I will do. Spare but my life, and I will entreat the king to restore these lands to your feudal lords, Llewelyn and Howel ap Res Vychan. It was by my doing that they were wrested from them. I confess it freely now. Grant me but my life, and I will undo the work I have done. I will restore to you your youthful chiefs. Again I swear it; and I have the ear of his Grace. If thou hast thy country's cause at heart thou wilt hear me in this thing. I will give you back the lords you all love. I will trouble you no more myself. I would I had never seen this evil place. It has been nought but a curse to me from the day it was bestowed."

The man uttered a harsh laugh, and stood as if considering.

Raoul, whose eyes never left the shining blade his foe held suspended in his hand, pleaded yet more and more eloquently, and, as it seemed, with some effect, for the soldier presently sheathed his weapon, and bid the wretched youth rise and follow him. Raoul obeying, soon found himself in the presence of a wild crew of Welsh kerns, who were holding high revelry in the banqueting hall, whilst his own English servants—those, at least, who had not effected their escape—lay dead upon the ground, the presence of bleeding corpses at their very feet doing nothing to check the savage mirth and revelry of the victors, who had been joined by the whole of the Welsh garrison, only too glad of an excuse for rising against the usurper.

A silence fell upon the company as the dark-bearded soldier marched his captive into the hall, the yell of triumph being hushed by commanding gesture from the captor. A long and unintelligible debate followed, Raoul only gathering from the faces of those present what were their feelings towards him. He stood cowering and quaking before that fierce assembly—a pitiful object for all eyes. But at length his captor briefly informed him that his terms were accepted: that if he would write his request to the king and obtain its fulfilment, he should go free with a whole skin; but that, pending the negotiation, which could be carried on by the fathers of the Abbey of Strata Florida, he would remain a close prisoner, and his ransom would be the king's consent.

These were the best terms the unhappy Raoul could obtain for himself, and he was forced to abide by them. The fathers of the abbey were honest and trustworthy, and carried his letters to the king as soon as they had penned them for him. Raoul was clever in diplomatic matters, and was so anxious for his own safety that he took good care not to drop a hint as to the evil conduct of the people of Iscennen, which might draw upon them the royal wrath and upon him instant death.

Evelyn Everett-Green

He simply represented that he was weary of his charge of this barren estate, that he preferred life in England and at the court, and found the revenues very barren and unprofitable. As the former owners had redeemed their character by quiet conduct during the past year and a half, his gracious Majesty, he hinted, might be willing to gratify them and their people by reinstating them.

And when Edward read this report, and heard the opinion of the father who had brought it—a wily and a patriotic Welshman, who knew how to plead his cause well—he made no trouble about restoring to Llewelyn and Howel their lands, only desiring that Wendot should renew his pledge for their loyalty and good conduct, and still hold himself responsible for his brothers to the king.

And so Llewelyn and Howel went back to Carregcennen, and Wendot and Griffeth remained at Dynevor, hoping with a fond hope that this act of clemency and justice on the part of Edward would overcome in the mind of the twins the deeply-seated hatred they had cherished so long.

CHAPTER IX

THE RED FLAME OF WAR

"Wendot, Wendot, it is our country's call! Thou canst not hang back. United we stand; divided we fall. Will the Prince of Dynevor be the man to bring ruin upon a noble cause, by banding with the alien oppressor against his own brethren? I will not believe it of thee. Wendot, speak—say that thou wilt go with us!"

Wendot was standing in his own hall at Dynevor. In the background was a crowd of retainers and soldiers, so eagerly discussing some matter of vital interest that the brothers stepped outside upon the battlemented terrace to be out of hearing of the noise of their eager voices.

There was a deep gravity on Wendot's face, which was no longer the face of a boy, but of a youth of two-and-twenty summers, and one upon whom the cares and responsibilities of life had sat somewhat heavily. The tall, well-knit frame had taken upon it the stature and developed grace of manhood; the sun-browned face was lined with traces of thought and care, though the blue eyes sparkled with their old bright and ready smile, and the stern lines of the lips were shaded and hidden by the drooping moustache of golden brown. There were majesty, power, and intellect

Evelyn Everett-Green

stamped upon the face of the young Lord of Dynevor, and it was very plain to all who observed his relations with those about him that he was master of his own possession, and that though he was greatly beloved by all who came in contact with him, he was respected and obeyed, and in some things feared.

By his side stood Griffeth, almost as much his shadow as of yore. To a casual observer the likeness between the brothers was very remarkable, but a closer survey showed many points of dissimilarity. Griffeth's figure was slight to spareness, and save in moments of excitement there was something of languor in his movements. The colour in his cheeks was not the healthy brown of exposure to sun and wind, but the fleeting hectic flush of long-standing insidious disease, and his eyes had a far-away look—dreamy and absorbed; whilst those of his brother expressed rather watchful observation of what went on around him, and resolution to mould those about him to his will.

Facing this fair-haired pair were the twin Lords of Iscennen, considerably changed from the sullen-looking lads of old days, but still with many of their characteristics unchanged. They were taller and more stoutly built than Wendot and Griffeth, and their dark skins and coal-black hair gave something of ferocity and wildness to their appearance, which look was borne out by the style of dress adopted, whilst the young Lords of Dynevor affected something of the refinement and richness of apparel introduced by the English.

For the past years a friendly intercourse had been kept up between Dynevor and Carregcennen. The country had been at peace—such peace as internal dissensions would allow it—and no one had disturbed the sons of Res Vychan in the possession of their ancestral rights. The tie between the brothers had therefore been more closely drawn, and Wendot's responsibility for the submissive behaviour of the turbulent twins had made him keep a constant eye upon them, and had withheld them on their side from attempting to foment the small and fruitless struggles against English authority which were from time to time arising between the border-land chief and the Lords of the Marches.

But now something very different was in the wind. After almost five years of peace with England, revolt had broken out in North Wales. David, the brother of Llewelyn, had commenced it, and the prince had followed the example thus set him. He had broken out into open rebellion, and had summoned the whole nation to stand by him in one united and gallant effort to free the country from the foreign foe, and unite it once again as an undivided province beneath the rule of one sovereign.

The call was enthusiastically responded to. North Wales rose as one man, and flocked to the banners of the prince and his brother. South Wales was feeling the contagion of coming strife, and the pulse of the nation beat wildly at the thought that they might win liberty by the overthrow of the foe. One after another the petty chiefs, who had sworn fealty to Edward, renounced their allegiance, and mustered their forces to join those of Llewelyn and David. The whole country was in a wild ferment of patriotic excitement. The hour seemed to them to have arrived when all could once again band together in triumphant vindication of their national rights.

Llewelyn and Howel ap Res Vychan were amongst the first to tender their allegiance to the cause, and, having sent on a compact band of armed men to announce their coming in person, had themselves hurried to Dynevor to persuade their brothers there to join the national cause.

Evelyn Everett-Green

And they found Wendot less indisposed than they had feared. The five years which had passed over his head since he had fallen under the spell of the English king's regal sway had a good deal weakened the impression then made upon him. Edward had not visited the country in person since that day, and the conduct of the English Lords of the Marches, and of those who held lands in the subjected country, was not such as to endear their cause to the hearts of the sons of Wales. Heart-burnings and jealousies were frequent, and Wendot had often had his spirit stirred within him at some tale of outrage and wrong. The upright justice of the king was not observed by his subjects, and the hatred to any kind of foreign yoke was inherently strong in these sons of the mountains. In the studies the Dynevor brothers had prosecuted together they had imbibed many noble thoughts and many lofty aspirations, and these, mingling with the patriotic instinct so strongly bound up in the hearts of Cambria's sons, had taught them a distrust of princes and an intense love for freedom's cause, as well as a strong conviction that right must ever triumph over might.

So when the news arrived that the north was in open revolt, it struck a chord in the hearts of both brothers; and when the dark-browed twins came with the news that they had openly joined the standard of Llewelyn, they did not encounter the opposition they had expected, and it was with an eager hopefulness that they urged upon the Lord of Dynevor to lend the strength of his arm to the national cause.

"Wendot, bethink thee. When was not Dynevor in the van when her country called on her? If thou wilt go with us, we shall carry all the south with us; but hang thou back, and the cause may be lost. Brother, why dost thou hesitate? why dost thou falter? It is the voice of thy country calling thee. Wilt thou not heed that call? O Wendot, thou knowest that when our parents lived—when they bid us not look upon the foe with too great bitterness—it was only because a divided Wales could not stand, and that submission to England was better than the rending of the kingdom by internal strife. But if she would have stood united against the foreign foe, thinkest thou they would ever have held back? Nay; Res Vychan, our father, would have been foremost in the strife. Are we not near in blood to Llewelyn of Wales, prince of the north? Doth not the tie of blood as well as the call of loyalty urge us to his side? Why dost thou ponder still? Why dost thou hesitate? Throw to the wind all idle scruples, and come. Think what a glorious future may lie before our country if we will but stand together now!"

Wendot's cheek flushed, his eye kindled. He did indeed believe that were his father living he would be one of the first to hasten to his kinsman's side. If indeed the united country could be strong enough to throw off the yoke, what a victory it would be! Was not every son of Wales bound to his country's cause at such a time?

There was but one thing that made him hesitate. Was his word of honour in any wise pledged to Edward? He had paid him homage for his lands: did that act bind him to obedience at all costs?

But such refinements of honour were in advance of the thought of the time, incomprehensible to the wilder spirits by whom he was surrounded. Llewelyn answered the brief objection by a flood of rude eloquence, and Howel struck in with another argument not without its weight.

"Wendot, whatever course thou takest thou art damned in Edward's eyes. Thou hast held thyself surety for us, and nought but death will hold us back from the cry of our country in her need. Envious eyes are cast already by the rapacious English upon these fair lands of thine, which these

Evelyn Everett-Green

years of peace have given thee opportunity to enrich and beautify. Let the king once hear that we have rebelled, and his nobles will claim thy lands, thy life, thy liberty, and thou must either yield all in ignominious flight or take up arms to defend thyself and thine own. I trow that no son of Res Vychan will stand calmly by to see himself thus despoiled; and if thou must fight, fight now, forestall the foe, and come out sword in hand at thy country's call, and let us fight shoulder to shoulder and hand to hand, as our forefathers have done before us. Thou knowest somewhat of English rule, now that thou hast lived beneath it these past years. Say, wilt thou still keep thy neck beneath the yoke, or wilt thou do battle like a warrior for liberty and independence? By our act thou art lost—yet not even that thought can hold us back—then why not stand or fall as a soldier, sword in hand, than be trapped like a rat in a hole in inglorious inaction? For methinks whatever else betided thou wouldst not raise thy hand against thy countrymen, even if thy feudal lord should demand it of thee."

"Never!" cried Wendot fiercely, and his quick mind revolved the situation thus thrust upon him whilst Howel was yet speaking.

He saw at once that a course of neutrality would be impossible to him. Fight he must, either as Edward's vassal or his foe. The first was impossible; the second was fraught with a keen joy and secret sense of exultation. It was true what Howel said: he would be held responsible for his brothers' revolt. The English harpies would make every endeavour to poison the king's mind, so that they might wrest from him his inheritance. He would be required to take up arms against his brothers, and his refusal to do so would be his death warrant. Disgrace and ruin lay before him should he abide by such a course. The other promised at least glory and renown, and perhaps a soldier's death, or, better still, the independence of his country—the final throwing off of the tyrant's yoke.

His heart swelled within him; his eyes shone with a strange fire. Only one thought checked the immediate utterance of his decision, and that was the vision of a pair of dark soft eyes, and a child's face in which something of dawning womanhood was visible, smiling upon him in complete and loving trust.

Yes, Wendot had not forgotten Gertrude; but time had done its work, and the image of the fair face was somewhat dim and hazy. He yet wore about his neck the half of the gold coin she had given him; but if he sometimes sighed as he looked upon it, it was a sigh without much real bitterness or regret. He had a tender spot in his memory for the little maid he had saved at the risk of his own life, but it amounted to little more than a pleasant memory. He had no doubt that she had long ago been wedded to some English noble, whose estates outshone those of Dynevor in her father's eyes.

During the first years after his return home he had wondered somewhat whether the earl and his daughter would find their way again to the rich valley of the Towy; but the years passed by and they came not, and the brief dream of Wendot's dawning youth soon ceased to have any real hold upon him. If her father had had any thoughts of mating her with the Lord of Dynevor, he would have taken steps for bringing the young people together.

The last doubt fled as Wendot thought this over; and whilst his brothers yet spoke, pointing to the rich stretch of country that lay before their eyes in all the glory of its autumn dress, and asking if that were not an inheritance worthy to be fought for, Wendot suddenly held out his hand, and said in clear, ringing tones:

Evelyn Everett-Green

"Brothers, I go with you. I too will give my life and my all for the liberty of our land. The Lord of Dynevor shall not be slack to respond to his country's call. Methinks indeed the hour has come. I will follow our kinsman whithersoever he shall bid."

Llewelyn and Howel grasped the outstretched hand, and from within the castle walls there burst forth the strains of wild melody from the harp of old Wenwynwyn. It seemed almost as though he must have heard the words that bound Wendot to the national cause, so exultant and triumphant were the strains which awoke beneath his hands.

It was but a few days later that the four brothers rode forth from beneath the arched gateway of Dynevor, all armed to the teeth, and with a goodly following of armed attendants. Wendot and Griffeth paused at a short distance from the castle to look back, whilst a rush of strange and unwonted emotion brought the tears to Griffeth's eyes which he trusted none saw beside.

There stood the grand old castle, his home from childhood—the place around which all the associations of a lifetime gathered. It was to him the ideal of all that was beautiful and strong and even holy—the massive walls of the fortress rising grandly from the rocky platform, with the dark background of trees now burning with the rich hues of autumn. The fair valley stretched before their eyes, every winding of which was familiar to them, as was also every individual tree or crag or stretch of moorland fell as far as eye could see. The very heart strings of Wendot and Griffeth seemed bound round these homelike and familiar things; and there was something strangely wistful in the glances thrown around him by the young Lord of Dynevor as he reined in his horse, and motioning to the armed followers to pass him, stood with Griffeth for a few brief moments alone and silent, whilst the cavalcade was lost to sight in the windings of the road.

"Is it a last farewell?" murmured the younger of the brothers beneath his breath. "Shall I ever see this fair scene again?"

And Wendot answered not, for he had no words in which to do so. He had been fully occupied all these last days—too much occupied to have had time for regretful thought; but Griffeth had been visiting every haunt of his boyhood with strange feelings of impending trouble, and his cheek was pale with the stress of his emotion, and his voice was husky with the intensity of the strain he was putting upon himself.

"Griffeth, Griffeth!" cried Wendot suddenly, "have I done wrong in this thing? I asked not thy gentle counsel, yet thou didst not bid me hold back. But tell me, have I been wrong? Could I have done other than I have?"

"I think not that thou couldst. This seems like a call from our country, to which no son of hers may be deaf. And it is true that our brothers have undone thee, and that even wert thou not willing to take up arms against them and thy countrymen, the rupture with Edward is inevitable. No, I am with thee in what thou hast done. The Lord of Dynevor must show himself strong in defence of his country's rights.

"Yet my heart is heavy as I look around me. For we are going forth to danger and death, and who knows what may betide ere we see these fair lands again, or whether we may ever return to see them more?"

Wendot would fain have replied with cheerful assurance, but a strange rush of emotion came over him as he gazed at his childhood's home, together with a sudden strong presentiment that there was something prophetic in his brother's words. He gazed upon the gray battlements and the brawling river with a passionate ardour in his glance, and then turning quickly upon Griffeth, he said:

"Brother, why shouldst thou leave it? thou art more fit for the safe shelter of home than for the strife of a winter war. Why shouldst thou come forth with us? Let us leave thee here in safety—"

"Wendot!"

It was but one word, but the volume of reproach compressed into it brought Wendot to a sudden stop. They looked into each other's eyes a moment, and then Griffeth said, with his sweet, meaning smile:

"We have never been separated yet, my Wendot; in sorrow and joy we have ever been together. It is too late to change all that now. I will be by thy side to the end. Be it for life or for death we will ride forth together."

And so with one hard hand clasp that spoke volumes, and with one more long, lingering look at the familiar towers of the old home, Wendot and Griffeth, the Lords of Dynevor, rode forth to meet their fate at the hands of the mighty English king.

Of that sudden, fierce, and partially successful revolt the history books of the age give account. Llewelyn and his brother David, joined by the whole strength of the North, and by much able assistance from the South, drove back the English across the border; and when Edward, hurrying to the spot, marched against them, his army was utterly routed near the Menai Straits, and the triumphant Welsh believed for a few brief months that they were victors indeed, and that the power of the foe was hopelessly broken.

Llewelyn with his army retired to the fastnesses of Snowdon, where the English durst not pursue them, and these less hardy soldiers suffered so terribly in the winter cold that the mortality in their ranks caused the triumphant mountaineers to prophesy that their work would be done for them without any more exertion on their part.

But the lion-hearted King of England was not of the stuff that easily submits to defeat. He knew well that Wales was in his power, and that he had but to exercise patience and resolution, and the final victory would be his.

Permitting no relaxation of his efforts in the North, even when the winter's bitter cold was causing untold sufferings amongst his soldiers, he commenced a muster of troops in the South, from which country most of the disaffected nobles had drawn away to join the insurgents under the Prince of Wales, as Llewelyn was called. It was a shock of no small magnitude to that prince to hear that his foe was thus employing himself; and leaving the fastnesses of Snowdon with a picked band of his hardiest men, amongst whom he numbered Llewelyn and Howel, he marched southward himself, hoping to overthrow this new force before it had gathered power sufficient to be dangerous.

Wendot would gladly have been of the number, for inaction, and the rude barbarism he saw around him, were inexpressibly galling to him; and the more he saw of the savage spirits by whom he was surrounded the less he was able to hope for any permanent advantage as the result of this rising. The jealousies of the respective chiefs were hardly held in check even in the face of a common peril. It was impossible not to foresee that the termination of a war with England would only be the signal for an outbreak of innumerable petty animosities and hostile feuds.

Evelyn Everett-Green

So Wendot would have been thankful to escape from this irksome inactivity, and to join the band going south; but the condition of Griffeth withheld him, for the youth was very ill, and he often felt that this winter of hardship up in the mountain air was killing him by inches, although he never complained.

It was out of the question for Griffeth to march or to fight. He lay most of the day beside a little fire of peat, in a cabin that Wendot and his men had constructed with their own hands, beneath the shelter of a rock which broke the force of the north wind, and formed some protection against the deep snow. Griffeth had borne his share gallantly in the earlier part of the campaign, but a slight wound had laid him aside; and since the intense cold had come, he had only grown more white and wasted and feeble day by day. Now that the sun was gaining a little more power, and that the melting of the snow bespoke that spring was at hand, Wendot began to hope the worst was over; but to leave his brother in such a state was out of the question, and he saw Llewelyn and Howel depart without attempting to join them.

Days and weeks had passed, and no news had been received by those up in the mountains of the result of Llewelyn's expedition. It was reported by scouts that Edward was at Carnarvon Castle in person, making hostile demonstrations of a determined kind, which, in the absence of their chief, the wild Welsh kerns knew not how to repel. They were safe where they were, and awaited the return of their leader; but a terrible stroke had yet to fall upon them, which proved the final blow to all their hopes and ambitions.

It was a wild, windy night. Wendot had piled the fire high, and was sitting with Griffeth talking of past days, and gazing with an unconscious wistfulness into the glowing embers, which seemed to him to take the semblance of those familiar towers and rocks which he sometimes felt as though he should never see again. Griffeth paused in the midst of something he was saying, and looked round with a start. It seemed to both brothers as though a hand was fumbling at the latch. Wendot rose and opened the door, and a tall, gaunt figure staggered rather than walked into the room, and sank down as if perfectly exhausted beside the glowing fire.

Griffeth uttered a startled exclamation.

"Llewelyn!" he cried sharply; and Wendot, barring the door, and coming forward like one in a dream, asked with the calmness of one who reads dire disaster:

"Where is Howel?"

"Dead," came the answer in a hollow voice, as though the speaker was exhausted past words—"dead by the side of Llewelyn our prince. Would that I too lay beside them!"

Wendot, too stunned to say another word at that moment, busied himself in getting his brother food and wine, of which he plainly stood sorely in need. He ate ravenously and in perfect silence; and his brothers watched him without having the heart to put another question. Indeed they knew the worst: their prince dead; the flower of their army slain—their own brother among the number—the rest dispersed; the remaining forces without a leader, without a rallying point, without a hope. What need of farther words?

Presently Llewelyn spoke again, this time with more strength, but still with the sullenness of despair:

"It was a mere skirmish on the banks of the Wye. We were in advance of the main body, and a party of English fell upon us. We did our best to sell our lives dearly. I thought I had sold mine when my time came, but I awoke and found myself beside the stream. Howel was lying upon me, stark and dead, and our prince a few yards away, with his own men round him. I do not think the foe knew whom they had slain, or they would have taken at least his head away as a trophy. I know not who took the news to our comrades, but they learned it, and dispersed to the four winds. I was forced to remain for some days in a shepherd's hut till my wounds were somewhat healed, and since then I have been struggling back here, not knowing what had befallen our camp in these mountains. Am I the first to bear the, news, or has it been known before?"

"You are the first," answered Wendot in a strange, blank voice. "We have heard nothing; we have been living in hopes of some triumph, some victory. We will let our fellows rest in peace one night longer. Tomorrow we must tell all, and decide what our action must be."

"There is nothing more to hope for," said Llewelyn darkly. "Our hope is dead, our last prince lies in a nameless grave. There is but one choice open to us now. Let those who will submit themselves to the proud usurper, and let us, who cannot so demean the name we bear, go forth sword in hand, and die fighting to the last for the country we may not live to deliver."

It seemed, indeed, as if Llewelyn's words were to prove themselves true; for no sooner did the news of the disaster on the banks of the Wye become known than the army began to melt away, like the snow in the increasing power of the sun. The chiefs, without a head, without a cause or a champion, either retired to their own wild solitudes or hastened to make their peace with their offended king; and only those who put honour before safety or life itself stood forth sword in hand to die, if it might be, with face to foe in defence of a cause which they knew was hopelessly lost.

And amongst this gallant but reckless little band were the three brothers of Dynevor, who, having once taken up the sword against Edward, were determined not to lay it down until the hand of death was cold upon each heart.

Evelyn Everett-Green

CHAPTER X

CARNARVON CASTLE

"There has been a battle—desperate fighting. They are bringing the prisoners into the guardroom," cried Britton, bursting into the royal apartments with small ceremony in his excitement. "Come, Alphonso; come, Joanna—let us go and see them. Our fellows say they made a gallant stand, and fought like veritable tigers. In sooth, I would I had been there. Methinks it is the last of the fighting these parts will see for many a long year."

Alphonso sprang up at the word of his comrade, eager to go and see the prisoners, his humane and kindly nature prompting him to ascertain that no undue harshness was displayed towards them by the rude soldiers. But Joanna, although her face was full of interest and eagerness, shook her head with a little grimace and a glance in the direction of her governess, Lady Edeline; for during the years that had elapsed between the visit of the royal children to Rhuddlan and this present visit to Carnarvon, Joanna had grown from a child to a woman, and was no longer able to run about with her brothers at will, though she still retained her old fearless, independent spirit and impulsive generosity of temperament, and was a universal favourite, despite the fact that she gave more trouble than any of her younger sisters.

The royal family had been for some time in Wales. They had wintered at Rhuddlan, where the little Princess Elizabeth had been born the previous year, just prior to the outbreak of the rebellion. Now they were at Carnarvon for greater security, the king considering that fortress the stronger of the two. The rebellion was practically at an end, but there was much to look into and arrange with regard to the rebels and their affairs, and there was the prospect of a considerable sojourn at the castle.

At this moment Edward was himself absent, though not far away. It had been rumoured that there had been sharp, irregular fighting all about the region of Snowdon, where the rebels had had their headquarters. Considerable excitement had prevailed for some time in the English ranks, and there was still complete uncertainty as to the fate of Llewelyn, Prince of Wales; for although a rumour was rife that he had fallen in fight, it had never been corroborated by trustworthy testimony, and so long as that turbulent prince remained alive there was no security for the peace or submission of the country.

Thus it was that the news of a victory and the capture of prisoners was exceedingly exciting to those within the castle. Alphonso, who was looking somewhat stronger for his sojourn in the bracing air of Wales, sprang up to go with Britton to make inspection, and again Joanna secretly bewailed her fate at being a girl, unable to take an equal share with her brother in such matters.

The guardroom at the castle was a vast and really fine apartment, with a vaulted roof and majestic pillars, that gave the idea of much rude strength of construction. Just at this moment it was the scene of an animated picture, and the boys paused at the door by which they had entered to look about them with eager curiosity.

Evelyn Everett-Green

The hall was full of soldiers, most of whom wore the English king's badge, and were known by sight to them as being attached to the castle; but mingled with these were other men, some in the English dress, but many others wearing the wild garb of the sons of the mountains, and these last had, for the most part, fetters on their wrists, or were bound two and two together and guarded by the English, whilst many of them were drooping under the effect of ghastly wounds, and several forms lay stretched along the ground indifferent to, or insensible of, their surroundings.

Desperate fighting there had been, indeed, to judge from appearances, and Alphonso's gentle spirit was stirred within him as he caught the sound of deep groans mingling with the loud voices of the soldiers. He had inherited the gentle spirit of his mother, and the generosity which always takes the part of the weak and oppressed. It mattered not that these men had been taken with swords drawn against his royal father; they were prisoners now, they had lost their all; and if rebels from the English standpoint, had been striving to free their country from what appeared to them as the unjust inroads of a foreign foe.

Alphonso, himself sinking into an early grave, and fully aware of his own state, saw life somewhat differently from his soldier sire, and felt little sympathy for that lust of conquest which was to the great Edward as the elixir of life. The lad's thoughts were more of that eternal crown laid up in the bright land where the sword comes not, and where the trump of war may never be heard. The glory of an earthly diadem was as nothing to him, and he had all that deep love for his fellow men which often characterizes those who know that their time on earth is short.

Stepping forward, therefore, with the air of quiet authority which he knew so well how to assume, he enforced silence by a gesture; and as the soldiers respectfully fell back before him, he walked through the groups of prisoners, speaking friendly words to them in their own tongue, and finally gave strict command to the captain of the guardroom to remove the fetters from those who were wounded, and see that they had all due tendance and care, whilst the rest were to be guarded with as little rigour as possible, and shut up together, where they would have at least the consolation of companionship in their misfortune.

The captain gave respectful heed to these words, and was by no means loath to carry out his instructions. He was a humane man himself, though inured to the horrors of war, and he, in common with all who came into contact with the young prince, felt towards him a great love and reverence; for there was something unearthly at times in the radiant beauty of the young Alphonso's face, and the growing conviction that he was not long for this world increased the loving loyalty shown to him by all.

"Your Grace's behests shall be obeyed," answered the man readily; "I myself will see that the wounded receive due and fitting care. They are brave fellows, be they rebels or no, and verily I believe there is not a man of them but would have laid down his life a hundred times to save that of the two young leaders who led them on to the last desperate sally. Such gallant feats of arms I have seldom beheld, and it was sore trouble to capture without killing them, so fiercely did they fight. But I bid the men take them alive, if possible, as they seemed too gallant and noble to fall in that vain struggle. Methinks, could they be tamed to serve the king as valiantly as they fought for that forlorn hope, they might be well worth the saving. I am always loath to see a brave life flung away, be it of friend or foe."

"Right, good Poleyn; thy words do thee credit. And where

are these gallant leaders? Show me them, for I would fain speak a kindly word to them. I would not that they feared my father's wrath too much. Stern he may be, but cruel never, and it would please me well to bid them submit themselves to him, that he might the more readily forgive them. Tell me which they be."

"They are not here," answered the captain; "I had them removed for greater comfort and security to mine own lodging. One of them is so sore wounded that I feared he would not live to make submission to the king unless he had prompt and skilful tendance; whilst the other, although his hurts be fewer and less severe, looks as if some mortal sickness were upon him. It may be nought but the feebleness that follows loss of blood and hard fighting; but I left them both to the care of my wife, who is the best tender of the sick that I have ever known. They came under her hands last night, brought on by our mounted fellows in advance of the rest. Today they are somewhat recovered; but I have had scarce time to think of them. I have been occupied since dawn with these other prisoners."

"I would fain see these youths; said you not they were but youths, Poleyn?" said Alphonso, whose interest was aroused by the tale he had heard. "I will go to your lodging and request admittance. Your worthy wife will not refuse me, I trow?"

The man smiled, and said that his wife would be proud indeed to be so visited. Alphonso, to whom the intricacies of the castle were well known, lost no time in finding the lodging of the captain of the guard, and quickly obtained admittance to the presence of the wounded youths, who occupied a comfortable chamber over the gateway, and had plainly been well looked to by the capable and kindly woman who called Poleyn her lord and master.

The bright light of day was excluded from the sickroom, and as the prince stood in the doorway his eyes only took in the general appearance of two recumbent figures, one lying upon a couch beside a glowing fire of wood, and the other extended motionless upon a bed in an attitude that bespoke slumber, his face bandaged in such a way that in no case would it have been recognizable.

But as Alphonso's eyes grew used to the darkness, and fixed themselves upon the face of the other youth, who was dressed and lying on the couch, he suddenly gave a great start, and advanced with quick steps to his side.

"Griffeth!" he cried suddenly.

The figure on the couch gave a start, a pair of hollow eyes flashed open, there was a quick attempt to rise, checked by the prince himself, and Griffeth exclaimed in the utmost astonishment:

"Prince Alphonso!"

"Yes, Griffeth, it is I indeed;" and then the prince sat down on the edge of the couch and gazed intently at the wasted features of the youth, towards whom in days gone by he had felt such a strong attachment.

There was something of sorrow and reproach in his glance as he said gently:

"Griffeth, can it really be thou? I had not thought to have seen thee in the ranks of our foes, fighting desperately against my father's soldiers. Whence has come this bitter change in thy feelings? and what is Wendot doing, who was to act as guardian toward his younger brethren? Hast thou broken away from his controlling hand? O Griffeth, I grieve to see thee here and in such plight."

But Griffeth's sad glance met that of the young prince unfalteringly and without shame, although there was something in it of deep and settled sorrow. He made a gesture as though he would have put out his hand, and Alphonso, who saw it, grasped it warmly, generous even when he felt that he and his father had been somewhat wronged.

"Think not that we took up arms willingly, Wendot and I," he said faintly, yet with clearness and decision. "Ay, it is Wendot who lies there, sore wounded, and sleeping soundly after a night of fever and pain. We shall not disturb him, he is fast in dreamland; and if you would listen to my tale, gentle prince, I trow you would think something less hardly of us, who have lost our all, and have failed to win the soldier's death that we went forth to seek, knowing that it alone could make atonement for what must seem to your royal father an act of treachery and breach of faith."

And then Griffeth told all his tale—told of the wrongs inflicted on hapless Wales in Edward's absence by the rapacious nobles he had left behind him to preserve order, of the ever-increasing discontent amongst the people, the wild hope, infused by David's sudden rising, of uniting once and for all to throw off the foreign yoke and become an independent nation again. He told of the action taken by their twin brothers, of the pressure brought to bear upon Wendot, of the vigilant hostility of their rapacious kinsman Res ap Meredith, son of the old foe Meredith ap Res, now an English knight, and eager to lay his hands upon the broad lands of Dynevor. It was made plain to the prince how desperate would have been Wendot's condition, thus beset with foes and held responsible for his brothers' acts. Almost against his will had he been persuaded, and at least he had played the man in his country's hour of need, instead of trying to steer his way by a cold neutrality, which would have ruined him with friend and foe alike.

Griffeth told of the hardships of that campaign amongst the mountains; of the death of Llewelyn the prince, and of his brother Howel; and of the resolve of the gallant little band, thus bereft of their hope, to go out and die sword in hand, and so end the miserable struggle that had ceased to be aught but a mockery of war. It was plainly a bitter thought even to the gentle Griffeth that they had not met the death they craved, but had fallen alive into the hands of the foe.

Alphonso gently chid him, and comforted him with brave and kindly words; and then he asked what had befallen his brother Llewelyn, and if he had likewise fallen in the fight.

"Nay; he was not with us when we made that last rally. He commenced the march with us, but his wound broke out again, and we were forced to leave him behind. He and a handful of faithful servants from Iscennen and Dynevor were to try and push on to the stronghold of Einon ap Cadwalader, and ask counsel and assistance from him. In old days he and our father were friends. Although he was one of the few who did not join Llewelyn in this rising, he has ever been well-disposed towards his countrymen. So we hoped our brother would find shelter and help there. If he had tried to march with us, he must assuredly have died."

"Ha!" said Alphonso smilingly, "methinks Llewelyn will have no trouble in gaining entrance there. Rememberest thou the Lady Arthyn, who was with us at Rhuddlan when thou wast there before? She hath left us of late to return to her father, whose loyalty has been proved, and whose request for his child was listened to graciously. But we shall be seeing them soon again, for my father betrothed Arthyn's hand to Raoul Latimer, whom doubtless thou rememberest as a somewhat haughty and quarrelsome lad. Time has softened down some of his rude tempers, and he has ever been eager for the match. My father has promised her hand in troth plight to him, and we await the coming of her and her father for the ceremony of betrothal.

"If I remember rightly, she was always a friend to thy brother. If so, he will find a ready welcome at her father's house, for my Lady Arthyn always had a soft spot in her heart for those we called rebels. She was a true daughter of Wales, albeit she loved us well, and she will like thy brother none the less that his sword has been unsheathed against the English usurper."

And then the prince and the rebel subject both laughed, and that laugh did more to bring them back to their old familiar relations than all that had gone before.

Griffeth was easily led on to tell the story of the life at Dynevor these past years; and Alphonso better understood from his unconscious self-betrayal than from his previous explanation how the fire of patriotic love burned in the hearts of these brothers. He thought that had he been one of them he would have acted even as they had done, and there was no anger but only a pitying affection in his heart towards one whose life was overshadowed by a cloud so like the one which hung upon the horizon of his own sky.

For it was plain to him that Griffeth's hold on life was very slight; that he was suffering from the same insidious disease which was sapping away his own health and strength. He had suspected it years before, and this supposition had made a link between them then; now he was certain of it, and certain, too, that the end could not be very far off. The fine constitution of the young Welshman had been undermined by the rigours of the past winter, and there was little hope that the coming summer would restore to him any of the fictitious strength which had long buoyed up Wendot with the hope that his brother would yet live to grow to man's estate.

"For myself I do not think I wish it," said Griffeth, with one of his luminous glances at Alphonso; "life is very hard, and there seems nothing left to live for. I know not how I could live away from the woods and rocks of Dynevor. But there is Wendot—my dear, kind, most loving brother. It cuts me to the heart to think of leaving him alone. Prince Alphonso, you are the king's son; will you pardon Wendot his trespass, and stand his friend with your royal father? I have no right to ask it. We have grievously offended, but he is my brother—"

A violent fit of coughing came on, and the sentence was never completed. Alphonso raised the wasted form in his arms, and soothed the painful paroxysm as one who knows just what will best relieve the sufferer. The sound roused Wendot, who had been sleeping for many hours, and although he had been brought in last night in an apparently almost dying state, his vigorous constitution was such that even these few hours' quiet rest, and the nourishment administered to him by the good woman who waited on him, had infused new life into his frame, so that he had strength to sit up in bed, and to push aside the bandage which had fallen over his eyes, as he anxiously asked his brother what was amiss.

Then Alphonso came towards him, and, holding his hand in a friendly clasp, told him that he had heard all the story, and that he was still their friend, and would plead for them with his father. Wendot, bewildered and astonished and ashamed, could scarce believe his senses, and asked, with a proud independence which raised a smile in Alphonso's eyes, that he might be led out to speedy death—the death by the headsman's axe, which was all he had now to hope for. Life had no longer any charms for him, he said; if only his young brother might be pardoned, he himself would gladly pay the forfeit for both.

But Alphonso, upon whose generous spirit bravery and self devotion, even in a foe, were never thrown away, replied kindly that he would see if peace could not be made with his offended sire, and that meantime Wendot must get well fast, and regain his health and strength, so as to be fit to appear before the king in person if he should be presently summoned.

But though the young prince left lighter hearts behind him in the room where the two eagles of Dynevor were imprisoned, he found that the task he had set himself with his father was a more difficult one than he had anticipated. Edward was very greatly incensed by this fierce and futile rebellion that had cost him so many hundreds of brave lives, and had inflicted such sufferings on his loyal troops. The disaster at Menai still rankled in his breast, and it was with a very stern brow and a face of resolute determination that he returned to Carnarvon to look into matters, and to settle upon the fate of the many prisoners and vassals who had once mere placed themselves or their lands in his sole power through the act which had rendered them forfeit.

Nor was Alphonso's task rendered less difficult from the fact that Sir Res ap Meredith had been before him, poisoning the king's mind against many of the Welsh nobles, and particularly against the sons of Res Vychan, in whose possession were the province and castle of Dynevor. Upon that fair territory he had long cast covetous eyes. He cared little in comparison for the more barren and turbulent region of Iscennen, and it was upon Wendot and Griffeth, but particularly upon Wendot, that the full bitterness of his invective was poured. He had so imbued the king with the idea that the youth was dangerous, turbulent, and treacherous (charges that his conduct certainly seemed to bear out), that it was small wonder if Edward, remembering his own former goodwill towards the youth, should feel greatly incensed against him. And although he listened to Alphonso's pleadings, and the lad told his story with much simple eloquence and fervour, the stern lines of his brow did not relax, and his lips set themselves into an ominous curve which the prince liked little to see.

"Boy," he said, with an impatience that boded ill for the success of the cause, "I verily believe wert thou in the place of king, thou wouldst give to every rebel chief his lands again, and be not contented until thine own throne came tottering about thine ears. Mercy must temper justice, but if it take the place of justice it becomes mere weakness. I trusted Wendot ap Res Vychan once, and laid no hand upon his lands. Thou hast seen how this trust has been rewarded. To reinstate him now would be madness. No. I have in Sir Res ap Meredith a loyal and true servant, and his claims upon his traitorous kinsman's lands may not be disregarded. Dynevor will pass away from Wendot. It is throwing words away to plead with me. My mind is made up. I trust not a traitor twice."

There was something in his father's tone that warned Alphonso to press the matter no more. He knew that when Edward thus spoke his word was final and irrevocable; and all he ventured now to ask was, "What will become of Wendot and his brother? You will not take their lives, sweet sire?"

"Their lives I give to thee, my son," answered Edward, with a gesture towards his boy which betrayed a deep love, and showed that although he had denied him sternly he did not

Evelyn Everett-Green

do so willingly. "As thou hast pleaded for them, I will not sentence them to death; but they remain my prisoners, and regain not their liberty. I know the turbulent race from which they spring. Sir Res will have small peace in his new possessions if any of the former princes of Dynevor are at large in the country. Wendot and Griffeth remain my prisoners."

"Nay, father; let them be my prisoners, I pray," cried Alphonso, with unwonted energy and animation. "Thou hast granted me their lives; grant me the keeping of their persons too. Nay, think not that I will connive at their escape. Give whatsoever charge thou wilt concerning the safety of their persons to those who guard us in our daily life, but let me have them as gentlemen of mine own. Call them prisoners an you will, but let their imprisonment be light—let me enjoy their company. Thou knowest that Britton is fretting for a freer life, and that I see little of him now. I have often longed for a companion to share my solitary hours. Give me Griffeth and Wendot. They have the royal blood of Wales flowing in their veins, and methinks they love me even as I love them. And, father, Griffeth has not many months, methinks, to live; and I know so well all he suffers that my heart goes out to him. He has the love of books that I have, and we have so many thoughts which none seem to understand save our two selves. And he and Wendot are as one. It would be cruelty such as thou wouldst not inflict to separate them whilst one has so short a time to live. Give me them for mine own attendants, and bid the servants guard them as best pleaseth thee. Sweet father, I have not asked many boons of thee. Grant me this one, I pray thee, for my heart is verily set on it."

There was something in this appeal, something in the look upon Alphonso's face, something in the very words he had used, that made it impossible to his father to refuse him. Blind his eyes as he would to the truth, he was haunted by a terrible fear that the life of his only son was surely slipping away. Alphonso did not often speak of his health, and the hint just dropped struck chill upon the father's heart. Passing his hand across his face to conceal the sudden spasm of pain that contracted it, he rose hastily from his chair, and said:

"Give thine own orders concerning these youths. I leave them in thy hands. Make of them what it pleaseth thee. Only let them understand that charge will be given to the custodians of the castle, and of whatever place they visit in the future, that they are prisoners at the king's pleasure, and that any attempt at escape will be punished with instant and rigorous captivity."

"So be it," answered Alphonso, with brightening eyes. "I thank thee, father, for the boon. Thou shalt never have cause to repent it."

Evelyn Everett-Green

CHAPTER XI

THE KING'S CLEMENCY

"Unhand me, sir. How dare you thus insult me? Let go my hand, or I summon help instantly. I am come to seek the king. Will you raise a tumult within hearing of his private apartments? Unhand me, I say," and Arthyn's cheeks flamed dangerously, whilst her eyes flashed fire.

But Raoul Latimer, though a craven before the face of an armed foe, could be resolute enough when he had only an unprotected woman to deal with, and was quite disposed to show his valour by pressing his unwelcome salutations upon the cheek of the girl he regarded as his future wife. His surprise at encountering Arthyn, whom he believed far away in her father's castle, hastening alone down one of the long corridors of Carnarvon Castle, had been very great. He could not imagine what had thus brought her, and was eager to claim from her the greeting he felt was his due.

But Arthyn had never lacked for spirit, and had always confessedly abhorred Raoul, nor had absence seemed to make the heart grow fonder, at least in her case. She repulsed him with such hearty goodwill that his cowardly fury was aroused, and had not the girl cried aloud in her anger and fear, he might have done her some mischief. But even as she lifted her voice a door in the corridor was flung open, and the king himself strode forth, not, as it chanced, in response to the call, which had not reached his ears, but upon an errand of his own. Now when he saw that at the doors of his own private apartments one of his own gentlemen had dared to lay rude hands upon a woman, his kingly wrath was stirred, and one blow from his strong arm sent Raoul reeling across the corridor till the wall stopped his farther progress.

"How now, malapert boy?" cried Edward in deep displeasure. "Is it thus you disgrace your manhood by falling upon the defenceless, and by brawling even within hearing of your sovereign? You are not so wondrous valiant in battle, Raoul Latimer, that you can afford to blast the small reputation you have.

"Sweet lady, be not afraid; thy king will protect thee from farther insult."

"Ha, Arthyn, is it thou, my child? Nay, kneel not in such humbly suppliant fashion; rise and kiss me, little one, for thou art only less dear to me than mine own children. Come hither, maiden, and speak to me. What has brought thee here alone and unannounced? And what has raised this storm betwixt ye twain?"

"Sire—my king—hear me," cried Arthyn in a choked voice; "and bid that wicked youth, whom I have ever hated, leave us. Let me speak to you alone and in private. It is to you, gracious lord, that I have come. Grant me, I pray you, the boon of but a few words alone and in private. I have somewhat to tell your grace—your royal pardon to ask."

"Pardon? tush, maiden! thou canst not have offended greatly. But come hither; what thou hast to say thou shalt say before the queen and Eleanor. They have ever been as mother and

Evelyn Everett-Green

sister to thee. Thou hast no secrets for me which they may not hear?"

"Ah no; I would gladly speak all before them," answered Arthyn eagerly, knowing that in the gentle Eleanor of Castile and her daughter she would find the most sympathizing of friends.

Intensely patriotic as the girl had ever been, loving her country above all else, and throwing heart and soul into that country's cause, she had yet learned a deep love and reverence for the family of the English king, amongst whom so many years of her young life had been spent. She was able to do full justice to the kindly and domestic side of the soldier king's nature, and, whilst she regarded him as a foe to Wales, looked upon him personally as a friend and protector.

Edward's gentleness and affection in his private life equalled his stern, unbending policy in matters of state. It was very tenderly and kindly that he led the girl to the private apartments of the queen; and when once Arthyn found herself face to face with one who had given to her more of mother love than any other being in the world, she flung herself into the arms opened to receive her, and out came the whole story which had brought her on this secret mission to Carnarvon.

"Sweet lady, O most gracious madam, listen and plead for me with the king. He is kind and good, and he knows what true love is. Lady, it is as a wedded wife I come to you, craving pardon for what I have done. But I ever hated that wicked Raoul Latimer, my country's foe, and would have died rather than plight my troth to him. And when he came to us—he, my love, my life, he whom I loved long years ago when we met as boy and girl, and whom I have never forgotten—what could I do? How could I resist?

"And my father approved. He gave my hand in wedlock. And now I am come to pray your pardon for myself and for him whom I love. Oh, do not turn a deaf ear to me! As you have loved when you were young, pardon those who have done likewise."

King and queen exchanged glances, half of amusement, half of astonishment, but there was no anger in either face. Raoul was no favourite in the royal circle, and his visible cowardice in the recent campaign had brought him into open disfavour with the lion-hearted Edward. He loved Arthyn dearly, and this proof of her independence of spirit, together with her artless confidence in his kindliness of heart, pleased him not a little. He had been forced during these past days to act a stern part towards many of the Welsh nobles who had been brought before him. He was glad enough, this thankless task accomplished, to allow the softer and more kindly side of his nature to assert itself. And perhaps the sympathetic glances of his son Alphonso, who had just entered the room, helped to settle his resolve that Arthyn at least should receive full and free forgiveness.

Eleanor had drawn her former playmate towards her, and was eagerly questioning her as to the name of him to whom her heart and hand were now given, and the answer sent a thrill of surprise through the whole company.

"It is one whom you all know, sweet Eleanor—Llewelyn, the son of Res Vychan, Lord of Dynevor. Thou knowest, Eleanor, how he came amongst us at Rhuddlan years agone now, and perchance thou sawest even then how we loved one another, albeit it was but the love of children. But we never have forgotten, and when he came to my father's castle, wounded and weary and despairing after the disaster which robbed Wales of her last native prince, what could we do but receive and tend him? It was thus it came about, and love did

Evelyn Everett-Green

the rest."

"And so thou hast wed a rebel, maiden?" quoth Edward, in tones that seemed to be stern by effort rather than by the will of the speaker, whilst the kindly light in the eyes belied his assumed harshness; "and having done so thou hast the hardihood to come and tell us of it thine own self. Fie upon thee for a saucy wench! What better dost thou expect for thyself and thy lord than a lodging in the lowest dungeon of the keep?"

"I know that we ought to expect nothing better," answered Arthyn, with her brightest smile, as she turned fearlessly upon the king. "But do as you will with us, noble king, and we will not rebel or complain, so that we may be together. And my dear lord bid me give you this. He took it with his own hands from the dead hand of Llewelyn, Prince of Wales, and he charged me to place it in your hands as a pledge and token that your enemy ceased to live. Report has told him that men say Llewelyn escaped that day, and that he yet lives to rise against you again. By this signet you may know that he lies dead and cold, and that with him has perished the last hope of Wales ever to be ruled by a prince of her own."

Edward put forth his hand eagerly, and examined the signet ring, which was one he himself had given to Llewelyn on the occasion of his last submission. And as he looked upon it a great weight seemed to be rolled from off him, for it was the first decided intimation he had had that his foe was actually slain. Rumour had been rife with reports of his escape, and although there had not been lacking testimony to the effect that the prince had fallen in battle, the fact had never been adequately established. A few quick questions to Arthyn appeared to establish this beyond all doubt, and in the expansion of the moment Edward was ready not only to forgive the bearer of such welcome tidings, but to forget that he had ever been an offender. One of the sons of Res Vychan had paid the price of his breach of faith with his life; two more were prisoners at his royal pleasure. Surely the family had suffered enough without harsher vengeance being taken. Surely he might give to Arthyn the liberty and possibly even the lands of her lord in return for the welcome intelligence she had brought.

Alphonso, ever on the side of mercy, joined with the queen and Eleanor in persuading the king to forgive and forget, and Arthyn was sent home the day following laden with presents and good wishes, bearing a full pardon to her lord from the English king, as well as a half promise that when the country became somewhat more settled he might make request for his commot of Iscennen with reasonable chance of being heard.

Wendot and Griffeth both saw their new sister before her return, and charged her with all sorts of friendly messages for Llewelyn. If Wendot thought it hard that the brother who had always been England's bitterest foe should be pardoned and rewarded, whilst he himself should be left to pine in captivity, at least he made no sign, and never let a word of bitterness pass his lips. Indeed he was too ill greatly to trouble himself over his own condition or the future that lay before him. Fever and ague had supervened upon the wounds he had received, and whilst Griffeth was rapidly recovering such measure of health and strength as he ever could boast, Wendot lay helpless and feeble, scarce able to lift his head from the pillow, and only just equal to the task of speaking to Arthyn and comprehending the good news with which she came charged.

The brothers had now been removed to better apartments, near to those occupied by the prince, whose servants they nominally were. Griffeth had begun to enter upon some of

Evelyn Everett-Green

his duties towards his royal patron, and the friendship begun in boyhood was rapidly ripening to an intimacy which surprised them both. Such perfect mutual understanding and sympathy was rare and precious; and Griffeth did not even look back with longing to the old life, so entirely had his heart gone out to the youthful prince, whose days on earth, like his own, were plainly numbered.

Lady Gertrude Cherleton was still an inmate of the royal household. She was now a ward of Edward's, her father having died a year or two previously. She was not considered a minor any longer, having attained the age of eighteen some time before, and the management of her estates was left partially to her. But she remained by choice the companion of Eleanor and Joanna, and would probably continue to do so until she married. It was a source of wonder to the court why she did not make choice of a husband amongst the many suitors for her hand; but she had hitherto turned a deaf ear to the pleadings of all. Sir Godfrey Challoner had long been sighing at her feet, but she would have none of him, and appeared to be proof against all the shafts of the blind god of love.

But her intense excitement when she heard of the arrival at Carnarvon of the two brothers from Dynevor told its own tale to the Princess Joanna, who had ever been the girl's confidante in this matter, and who had known from childhood how Gertrude had always believed herself pledged. It was a charming secret for them to cherish between them; and now that Wendot was once more beneath the castle roof, the impulsive Joanna would launch out into extravagant pictures of future happiness and prosperity. Her ardent temperament, having no personal romance to feed upon—for though her hand had once been plighted, her future lord had been drowned the previous year in a boating accident, and she was again free—delighted to throw itself into the concerns of her friend, and the sense of power which had been so early implanted within her made her confident of being able to overcome obstacles and attain the object of her wishes, be the difficulties and dangers in their path never so great.

"You shall be united, Gertrude, an he loves thee," cried the generous Joanna, flinging her arms round the neck of her companion, and kissing her again and again. "His life, his liberty, shall be obtained, and thou and he shall be happy together. I have said it, and I will do it."

Whatever was known to Joanna was known to Alphonso, who shared all her feelings, and was most tenderly beloved by her. He was as ardent in the cause as his sister could be; but he saw more of the difficulties that beset their path, and knew better his father's iron temperament, and how deeply Wendot had offended. Doubtless much was due to the misrepresentations of Sir Res ap Meredith, who had now secured for himself the coveted lands of Dynevor; but whatever the cause, the eldest son of the house of Dynevor was the object of the king's severe displeasure, and it was not likely he would relax his vigilance or depart from his word, not even for the prayers of his children or the tears of his favourite Gertrude. He had pardoned Llewelyn at the instance of Arthyn; if the same game were to be played over again by another of his daughters' companions, he would not unnaturally believe that he was being cajoled and trifled with.

"If it were only Griffeth it would be easy," said Alphonso thoughtfully. "But Wendot—"

And there he stopped and shook his head.

It was some days before the king saw the new attendant of his sons; but coming into Alphonso's private apartment one day suddenly, he found several of the royal children gathered

Evelyn Everett-Green

there, and with them a fair-haired youth, who was reading to the prince out of an illuminated missal. Alphonso was lying on a couch, and his look of fragile weakness struck cold to the father's heart. Of late the lad's strength had been failing rapidly, but Edward had tried to blind his eyes to the truth. Now he took a hasty step towards the couch, and Griffeth rose quickly from his seat and bent the knee before the king.

"Ha, Wendot," said Edward, with a grave but not unkindly glance, "I have not seen you at these new duties before. So you are a student as well as a soldier? Well, the arts of peace will better become you for the future. I remember your face well, young man. I would it had not been my duty to place you under restraint; but you have broken faith with me, and that grievously. How then can it be possible to trust you in the future? You, as the head of the house, should have set your brothers an example of honour and fealty. As it is, it has been far otherwise, and now you will have to bear the burden of that breach of trust and honour."

Twice Griffeth had opened his lips as if to speak, but Alphonso laid his hand upon his arm with a warning touch, which said as plainly as words could do, "Be silent."

So the youth held his peace, and only bent his head in submission; and Edward, after a moment's pause, added more kindly:

"And how fares it with your brother, Wendot? I hear that his state is something precarious. I hope he has the best tendance the castle can afford, for I would not that any member of my son's household should suffer from lack of care."

"He has all that he needs, I thank you, sire," answered Griffeth. "He lies sorely sick at this present time, but I trust he will amend ere long."

And then the king turned to his son, and spoke with him on some message of the state, and departed without heeding the excited glances of Joanna or the restless way in which she kept looking first at Alphonso and then at Gertrude.

But scarcely had the door closed behind the retiring form of the king before the excitable girl had bounded to her brother's side.

"O Alphonso," she cried, "did you do it on purpose? Tell me what you have in your head."

Alphonso sat up and pushed the hair out of his eyes. Griffeth was simply looking on in surprise and bewilderment. The prince laid a hand upon his arm and spoke very earnestly.

"Griffeth," he said, "it seems to me that through this error of my father's we may yet find means to compass the deliverance of Wendot. There are none of those save ourselves who know which of you twain is the first-born and which the youngest. In your faces there is little to mark you one from the other. Griffeth, if thou wilt be willing to be called Wendot—if Wendot will consent to be Griffeth—then we may perchance make his way plain to depart and live in liberty once more; for it is Wendot, and not Griffeth, who has so roused my father's anger. Griffeth he might easily consent to pardon; but Wendot he will keep as a hostage in his own hands possibly for life itself."

Griffeth listened, and a strange look crept into his face. His cheek flushed, and his breath came thick and fast. He knew Alphonso's motive in suggesting this change of identity. The lads, so closely drawn together in bonds of more than brotherly love, had not opened to each other their innermost souls for nought. Alphonso knew that no freedom, no liberty, would give to the true Griffeth any extension of his brief

Evelyn Everett-Green

span of life. His days were as assuredly numbered as those of the royal lad himself, and life had ceased to have attractions for the pair, whose spirits were almost on the wing, who had set their hopes and aspirations higher than anything which earth could give, and whose chiefest wish now was to remain together until death should call them home.

Griffeth's only trouble had been the thought of leaving his brother, and it was when he had realized from Alphonso's words that the king was deeply offended with Wendot, and that it was almost hopeless to think of his obtaining his liberty again, that the heart of the lad sank in despondency and sorrow.

For one of the young eagles of Dynevor thus to be caged—to be left to pine away in hopeless captivity, his brother gone from him as well as the prince who would stand his friend; possibly incarcerated at last in some dreary fortress, there to linger out his days in hopeless misery and inaction—the thought had been so terrible to Griffeth that there had been moments when he had almost longed to hear that the leeches gave up hope of saving his brother's life.

But Wendot was mending now; there was no doubt of ultimate recovery. He would rise from his sickbed to find— what? Griffeth had not dared to ask himself this question before; but now a great hope possessed him suddenly. He looked into Alphonso's eyes, and the two instantly understood one another; as did also Gertrude and Joanna, who stood by flushed and quivering.

"Let it be so," said Griffeth, in a voice which trembled a little, although the words were firm and emphatic. "I take the name the king has given me. I am Wendot, whom he believes the traitor and the foe. Griffeth lies yonder, sick and helpless, a victim to the influence of the first-born son of Res

Vychan. It may be, when the king hears more of him, he will in his clemency release and pardon him.

"Ah, if I could but be the means of saving my brother—the brother dearer to me than life—from the fate which others have brought upon him, that I could lay down my life without a wish ungratified! It has been the only thought of bitterness in my cup that I must leave him alone—and a prisoner."

Gertrude's face had flushed a deep red; she put out her hand and clasped that of Griffeth hard; there was a little sob in her voice as she said:

"Oh, if you will but save him—if you will but save him!"

Griffeth looked into her sweet face, with its sensitive features and soft eyes shining through a mist of tears, and he understood something which had hitherto been a puzzle to him.

There had been days when the intermittent fever from which Wendot suffered left him entirely for hours together, sometimes for a whole day; and Griffeth had been sure that on some of these days, in the hours of his own attendance on the prince, his brother had received visits from others in the castle: for flowers had appeared to brighten the sick room, and there had been a wonderful new look of happiness in the patient's eyes, although he had said nothing to his brother as to what had befallen him.

And in truth Wendot was half disposed to believe himself the victim of some sweet hallucination, and was almost afraid to speak of the fancies that floated from time to time before his eyes, lest he should be told that his mind was wandering, and that he was the victim of delusion.

Evelyn Everett-Green

Not once alone, but many times, during the hours of his tardy convalescence, when he had been lying alone, crushed by the sense of weariness and oppression which illness brings to one so little accustomed to it, he had been roused by the sound of light footfalls in his room; he had seen a graceful form flitting about, bringing lightness and beauty in her wake, and leaving it behind when she left. The vision of a sweet, small face, and the lustrous dark eyes which had haunted him at intervals through the long years of his young manhood, appeared again before him, and sometimes his name was spoken in the gentle tones which had never been forgotten, although the memory was growing dim.

Weak and dazed and feeble, both in body and mind, from the exhausting and wasting illness that had followed the severe winter's campaign, Wendot knew not if this vision was but the figment of his own brain, or whether the passionate love he felt rising up in his heart was lavished upon a mere phantom. But so long as she flitted about him he was content to lie and watch her, with the light of a great happiness in his eyes; and once when he had called her name—the never forgotten name of Gertrude—he had thought that she had come and taken his hand and had bent over him with a wonderful light in her eyes, but the very effort he made to rise up and grasp her hands, and learn if indeed it were a creature of flesh and blood, had resulted in a lapse back into unconsciousness, and he was silent as to the vision even to Griffeth, lest perchance he should have to learn that it was but a fevered dream, and that there was no Gertrude within the castle walls at all.

But Gertrude knew all; it was no dream to her. She saw the love light in the eyes dearest to her in the world. She had heard her name called; she had seen that the love she had cherished for the hero of her childhood had not been cherished in vain. Perhaps Wendot had betrayed more in his sickness and weakness than he would have allowed himself to do in his strength, knowing himself a helpless, landless prisoner in the hands of the stern monarch who occupied England's throne. But be that as it may, Gertrude had read his secret and was happy, though with such a chastened happiness as alone was possible to one who knew the peril in which her lover lay, and how hopeless even Alphonso thought it to obtain for him the king's pardon.

"My father would have betrothed us as children," said Gertrude, her face glowing, but her voice steady and soft, for why should she be ashamed of the faithful love of a lifetime?

"When we saw each other again he would have plighted us, but for the fear of what Llewelyn and Howel would do. But think you I love him less for his love to his country? Think you that I have aught to reproach him with, when I know how he was forced into rebellion by others? I care not what he has done. I love him, and I know that he loves me. Sooner would I share a prison with him than a palace with any man beside; yet I fear that in prison walls he will pine and die, even as a caged eagle, and it is that fear which breaks my heart.

"O Griffeth, Griffeth, if you can save him, how we will bless you from, our hearts! Give him to me, and I will guard and cherish him. I have wealth and lands for us both. Only his liberty is lacking—"

"And that we will strive to compass yet," said Alphonso gently. "Fear not, sweet Gertrude, and betray not thyself. Only remember from this time forward that Wendot is my friend and companion here, and that thy lover Griffeth lieth in yon chamber, sick and stricken."

"I will remember," she answered resolutely; and so the

change of identity was accomplished, with the result that the old chroniclers aver that Wendot, eldest son of Res Vychan, died in the king's prison in England, whilst all that is known of the fate of Griffeth is that he was with his brother in captivity in England in the year 1283, after which his name completely disappears, and no more is known of him, good or bad.

That night there were commotion and distress in Carnarvon Castle, for the young Alphonso broke a blood vessel in a violent fit of coughing, and for some hours his life was in the utmost danger.

The skill of the leeches, however, combined with the tender care of his mother and sisters, averted for a time fatal consequences, and in a few days the prince was reported to be out of immediate danger. But the doctors all agreed that it would not be wise for him to remain longer in the colder air of north Wales, and advised an immediate removal to Windsor, where more comforts could be obtained, and where the climate was milder and more genial.

Edward's work in Wales was done. The country was quiet, and he had no longer any fear of serious rebellion. The first thought in his mind was the precarious condition of his son, and immediate steps were taken to convey the invalid southward by slow and gentle stages.

A horse litter was prepared for him, and by his own special request this easy conveyance was shared by him with the two Welsh youths, to whom, as his father and mother thought, he had taken one of those strange sick fancies not uncommon to those in his state of health.

Wendot, as he called the younger brother, had been his most devoted nurse during the days of peril, and his quick understanding of the unspoken wishes of the prince had evoked a real and true gratitude from the royal parents.

The real Wendot was by this time so far recovered as to be able to bear the journey, and illness had so wasted him that he looked no older than Griffeth; and though still perplexed at being called Griffeth, and by no means understanding his brother's earnest request that he would continue to answer to the name, he was too weak to trouble his head much about the matter; and the two Welsh brothers were regarded by the English attendants as too insignificant to be worthy of much notice. The prince's freak to have them as travelling-companions was humoured by his parents' wish; but they little knew how much he was wrapped up in the brothers, nor how completely his heart was set upon seeing the accomplishment of his plan before he died.

Alphonso had all his senses about him, and the wistful look on Griffeth's face, as the mountains of his beloved Wales grew dim in the distance, was not lost upon him. Wendot was sleeping restlessly in the litter, and Alphonso stretched out his hand, and laid it gently upon Griffeth's.

"Art regretting that thou leavest all for me?" he asked gently; and the answer was such a look of love as went to his very heart.

"Nay; I would leave far more than that for thee, sweet prince, but it is my last look at home. I shall see these grand, wild hills no more."

"No, nor yet I," answered the prince, his own eyes growing somewhat dim; "and I, too, have loved them well, though not as thou lovest, my friend. But be content; there are fairer things, sweeter scenes than even these, in store for us somewhere. Shall we repine at leaving the beauties of earth, when the pearly gates of Paradise are opening before our very eyes?

"O Griffeth, it is a wondrous thought how soon we may be soaring above the very stars! And methinks it may well be given to thee to wing thy way to thine own home for one last look ere thou departest for the holy land whence we can never wish to return."

Griffeth gave him a bright, eager look.

"I will think that myself—I will believe it. This is not my last farewell."

CHAPTER XII

A STRANGE BRIDAL

"My prince, tempt me not. It is hard to refuse; but there are some things no man may do with honour, and, believe me, honour is dearer to me than life, dearer even than liberty; though Heaven alone knows how dear that is to every freeborn son of Cambria. I to leave my brother to wear away his days in captivity whilst I escape under his name! Prince Alphonso, I know not what you think my heart is made of. Am I to live in freedom, whilst he whom I love best in the world bears the burden of my fault, and lingers out his young life within the walls of the king's prison?"

Alphonso looked searchingly in Wendot's face, and realized for the first time the youth's absolute ignorance of his brother's state. No wonder he refused with scorn the proffered boon! Yet it would be a hard task to break the sad tidings to one who so deeply loved his gentle younger brother, from childhood his chosen comrade.

Alphonso was lying on a couch in one of the smaller state apartments of Windsor Castle, and the window, close to which he had bidden his attendants wheel him, overlooked the beautiful valley of the Thames. The first of the autumn tints were gilding the rich stretches of woodland, whilst a

Evelyn Everett-Green

faint blue haze hung over the distance, and the river ran like a silver thread, glinting here and there into golden brightness as some brighter ray of sunlight fell upon it.

Alphonso loved the view commanded by this window. He and Griffeth spent many long happy hours here, looking out on the fair prospect, and exchanging whispered thoughts and bright aspirations with regard to some land even fairer than the one they now beheld.

But Wendot never looked at the beautiful valley without experiencing a strange oppression of spirit. It reminded him of that wilder valley of the Towy, and his eyes would grow dim and his heart sick with the fruitless longing after home, which grew harder and harder to hear with every week of captivity, now that his bodily health was restored. Captivity was telling upon him, and he was pining as an eagle pines when caught and shut up by man even in a gilded cage. He looked pale and wan and wistful. Often he felt stifled by the warm, close air of the valley, and felt that he must die did he not escape to the freer air of the mountains.

But he seldom spoke of these feelings even to Griffeth, and strangely enough his illness and these homesick longings produced upon his outer man an effect which was wonderfully favourable to the plan fermenting in the brains of the royal children and their immediate companions.

Wendot had lost the sturdiness of figure, the brown colouring, and the strength of limb which had distinguished him in old days from Griffeth. A striking likeness had always existed between the brothers, whose features were almost identical, and whose height and contours were the same. Now that illness had sharpened the outlines of Wendot's face, had reduced his fine proportions, and had given to him something of the hollow-eyed wistfulness of expression which Griffeth had so long worn, this likeness became so remarkable that few in the castle knew one brother from the other. Knowing this, they both answered indifferently to the name of either, and any change of personality would be managed without exciting the smallest fear of remark.

Wendot had been perplexed at times by the persistence with which he had been addressed as Griffeth, even when he was certain that the speaker was one of the few who knew him and his brother apart; but he had not troubled his head much over the matter until this day, when Alphonso had openly spoken to him of the plan that was in their minds, and had bidden him prepare for a secret flight from the castle, promising that there should be no ardent search after him, as Wendot, and not Griffeth, was the culprit who had fallen under the royal displeasure, and the king would care little for the escape of the younger brother so long as he held the ex-Lord of Dynevor in his own safe keeping.

Wendot's indignant refusal to leave his brother and make good his own escape showed Alphonso how little he realized Griffeth's condition, and with gentle sympathy, but with candour and frankness, he explained to the elder brother how short would be the period of Griffeth's captivity—how soon and how complete the release for which he was patiently and happily waiting.

Wendot gave a great start as the meaning of Alphonso's words first broke upon him, and then he buried his face in his hands, and sat motionless, neither answering nor moving. Alphonso looked at him, and by-and-by put out his own wasted hand and laid it upon Wendot's knee.

"Does it seem a sad thing to thee, Wendot? Believe me, there is no sadness for Griffeth in the thought. Nay, is it not a blessed thing to know that soon, very soon, we shall be free

Evelyn Everett-Green

of this weary burden of pain and sickness and weakness, and laying all aside will pass away to the land of which the seer of old foretold that 'the wicked cease from troubling, and the weary are at rest.' Thou knowest not, perhaps, the sweetness of those words, but I know it well, and Griffeth likewise.

"Nay, Wendot, thou must learn not to grudge him the rest and the bliss of yon bright land. In this world he could look for nothing save wearing weakness and lingering pain. Thou shouldst be glad that the fiat has gone forth, and that the end may not be far off—the end of trouble and sorrow; for of the glory that shall follow there shall be no end."

But Wendot broke in hoarsely and impetuously.

"If he must die, let him at least die in freedom, with the old hills around him; let him be laid to rest beneath their shadow. You say that he might well escape; that no cry would be made after him so long as I were in the king's safe keeping. Let him then fly. Let him fly to Llewelyn and Arthyn. They will give him tendance and a home. He shall not die in prison, away from all that he holds dear. I cannot brook the thought!"

"Nay, Wendot," answered Alphonso with a kindling smile, "thou needest not grieve for thy brother because that he is here. Ask him—take it not from my lips; but I will tell thee this, that where thou art and where I am is the place where Griffeth would fain end his days. Ah! thou canst not understand, good youth, how when the great and wonderful call comes for the human soul, how lightly press the fetters of the flesh; how small these things of time and place appear that erst have been of such moment. Griffeth and I are treading the same path at the same time, and I think not even the offer of a free pardon and unfettered liberty would draw him from my side.

"Moreover, Wendot, he could not take the journey of which thou speakest. The keen autumn air, which will give thee strength and vigour, would but lay him low on the bed from which he would never rise. His heart is here with me. Think not that thou art wronging him in taking his name. The one load lying now upon his heart is the thought that he is leaving thee in captivity. Let him but know that thou art free—that he has been thy helper in thy flight—and he will have nought left to wish for in this world. His soul will be at peace."

Wendot rose and paced through the chamber, and then returned to the side of the prince. His face betrayed many conflicting emotions. He spoke with bitterness and impetuosity.

"And what good is life to me if I take you at your word and fly this spot? Have I not lost all that makes life worth living? My lands given to my traitorous kinsman; the brother who has been more to me than life lying in a foreign grave. What use is life to one so lonely and bereft? Where should I fly? what should I do? I have never lived alone. I have always had another to live for and to love. Methinks death would be the better thing than such a loveless life."

"And why should thy life be loveless, Wendot?" asked Alphonso, with kindling eyes and a brightening smile. "Dost not thou know?—does not thine own heart tell thee that one faithful heart beats for thee and thee alone? Have I not seen thee with her times and again? Have not your eyes told eloquent secrets—though I know not what your lips have said—"

Wendot's face was all in a glow, but he broke in hastily:

"Prince, prince, speak not of her. If I have been beguiled, if I

Evelyn Everett-Green

have betrayed the feelings which I cannot help, but which I must hold sternly in check—be not thou the one to taunt me with my weakness. There is none like her in the world. I have known it for long. But even because I know it so well I may not even dream of her. It is not with me as of old, when her father spoke to me of troth plight. I am a beggar, an outcast, a prisoner. She is rich, honoured, courted. She is the brightest star of the court—"

"And she loveth thee, Wendot," interposed Alphonso firmly. "She has loved thee from childhood with a faithful and true love which merits better things than to be cast aside as if it were but dross. What are lands and gold to a woman if her lover share them not? Is it meet that she should suffer so cruelly simply because her father has left her well endowed? Wendot, on Lord Montacute's dying bed this daughter of his avowed her love for thee, and he gave her his blessing and bade her act as she would. Art thou, then, to be the one to break her heart, ay, and thine own, too, because thou art too proud to take more than thou canst give?

"Fie, man! the world is wide and thou art young. Thou hast time to win thy spurs and bring home noble spoil to lay at thy lady's feet. Only let not pride stand in the way of her happiness and thine own. Thou hast said that life is dark and drear unless it be shared with some loved one. Then how canst thou hold back, when thou hast confessed thine own love and learned that hers is thine? Take it, and be grateful for the treasure thou hast won, and fear not but that thou wilt bring as much as thou wilt receive. There are strange chances in the fate of each one of us. Who knows but that thou and she will not yet reign again in the halls of Dynevor?"

Wendot started and flushed, and again paced down the whole length of the room. When he returned to the window Alphonso had gone, and in his place stood Gertrude herself, her sweet face dyed rosy red with blushes, her hands half stretched out towards him, her lips quivering with the intensity of her emotion.

He paused just one moment looking at her, and then holding out his arms, he said:

"Gertrude!"

Next moment she was clasped in his close embrace, and was shedding happy tears upon his shoulder.

"Oh!" said Gertrude at last, in a soft whisper, "it was worth waiting for this. I never thought I could have been so happy."

"Joanna—Alphonso, it is all settled. He will leave the castle with me. He will help me now in the care of my lands. But he will not move whilst Griffeth lives. And I think he is right. They have so loved each other, and he will not leave his brother to die amongst strangers in captivity."

"It is like him," said Joanna eagerly. "Gertrude, thou hast found a very proper knight, as we told thee from the first, when he was but a lad, and held the Eagle's Crag against a score of men. But ye must be wedded soon, that there be no delay when once the poor boy be gone. Every day he looks more shadowy and frail. Methinks that our softer air ill suits him, for he hath dwindled to a mere shadow since he came. You will not have to wait long."

"Joanna speaks the truth," said Alphonso, half sadly, half smilingly. "He will not be with us long. But it is very true that this marriage must be privately celebrated, and that without delay, that when the day comes when 'Griffeth' flies from the castle, he and his wife may go together."

"Ay, and my chaplain will make them man and wife, and breathe not a word to any man," cried Joanna, who, now that she was older, had her own retinue of servants, equal in number to those of her sister, by whom she was dearly loved for her generosity and frankness, so that she could always command ready and willing obedience to any expressed wish of hers.

"You think he will? O Joanna, when shall it be?"

"It shall be at midnight in the chapel," said the girl, with the prompt decision which characterized her. "Not tonight, but three nights from this. Leave all things in my hands, sweet Gertrude; I will see that nought is lacking to bind thee lawfully to thy lord. My chaplain is a good and holy man from the west country. He loveth those poor Welsh who are prisoners here, and spends much of his time in ministering to them. He loves thy future lord and his dying brother, and he knows somewhat of our plan, for I have revealed it in the confessional, and he has not chided me for it.

"Oh, I can answer for him. He will be glad that thou shouldst find so proper a knight; and he is kind of heart, and stanch to my service. Fear not, sweet Gertrude: ere three days have gone by thou shalt be a wedded wife; and when the time comes thou mayest steal away with him thy plighted lord, and trust thy sister Joanna to make thy peace with the king, if he be in any way angered or grieved."

Gertrude threw herself into Joanna's arms and kissed her a hundred times; and Joanna laughed, and said she deserved much credit for plotting to rid herself of her dearest friend, but was none the less loyal to the cause because Gertrude's gain would be her loss.

So there came a strange night, never to be forgotten by those who witnessed the proceedings, when Wendot ap Res Vychan and the Lady Gertrude Cherleton stood at midnight before the altar in the small private chapel of the castle, whilst the chaplain of the Princess Joanna's private suite made them man and wife according to the law of the Church. And of the few spectators who witnessed the ceremony two were of royal blood—Alphonso and Joanna—and beside them were only one or two attendants, sworn to secrecy, and in full sympathy with the youthful lovers thus plighting their troth and being united in wedlock at one and the same time.

Griffeth was not of the number who was present to witness this ceremony. He was unable to rise from his bed, a sudden access of illness having overtaken him, possibly as the result of the excitement of hearing what was about to take place.

When the solemn words had been spoken, and the bride was led away by her proud and happy spouse—happy even in the midst of so much peril and sorrow in the thought of the treasure he had won—she paused at the door of her apartments, whither he would have left her (for so long as they remained within the walls of the castle they would observe the same manner of life as before), and glancing into his face said softly:

"May I not go with thee to tell the news to Griffeth?"

"Ay, well bethought," said Alphonso, who was leaning on Wendot's other arm, the distance through the long passages being somewhat fatiguing to him. "Let us go and show to him thy wife. None will rejoice more than he to know that she is thine in very truth, and that none can take her from thee."

Griffeth's room was nigh at hand, and thither Wendot led his bride. A taper was burning beside the bed, and the sick youth lay propped up with pillows, his breath coming in laboured gasps, though his eyes were bright and full of comprehension as Wendot led the slim, white-robed figure to his side.

But the elder brother was startled at the change he saw in his patient since he had left him last. There was something in his look that struck chill upon his heart. He came forward and took the feeble hand in his. It was deadly cold, and the unearthly radiance upon the lad's face was as significant in its own way. Had not their mother looked at them with just such a smile when she had slipped away into another world, whilst they were trying to persuade themselves that she was better?

"My sister Gertrude," whispered Griffeth. "Oh, I am so happy! You will be good to him—you will comfort him.

"Wendot—Gertrude—" he made a faint effort, and joined their hands together; and then, as if his last earthly task was accomplished, he seemed to look right on beyond them, whilst a strange expression of awe and wonder shone from his closing eyes.

"Howel," he whispered—"father—mother—oh, I am coming! Take me with you."

Then the head fell backwards, the light vanished from the eyes, the cold hand fell nervelessly from Wendot's grasp, and they knew that Griffeth was the king's prisoner no longer.

Three days later the Lady Gertrude Cherleton said farewell to her royal companions, and started forth for her own estates in Derbyshire, which she had purposed for some time to visit. Perhaps had the minds of those in the castle been free to wonder at anything so trivial as the movements of the young heiress, they would have felt surprise at her selecting this time to betake herself to a solitary and independent existence, away from all her friends and playmates; but the mortal illness of the Prince Alphonso occupied the whole attention of the castle. The remains of the so-called Wendot, late of Dynevor, had been laid to rest with little ceremony and no pomp, and the very existence of the other brother was almost forgotten in the general dismay and grief which permeated through all ranks of people both within and without the castle walls.

The lady had a small but sufficient retinue; but it was considered rather strange that she should not start until the dusk had begun to gather round the castle, so that the confusion of the start was a good deal increased from the darkness which was stealing upon the place. Had there been much time or attention free, it might have been noted by a keen observer that Lady Gertrude had added to her personal attendants one who looked like a tall and stout woman, though her hood was so closely drawn that her face was seen by none of the warders, who, however, let her pass unchallenged: for she rode beside her mistress, and was evidently in the position of a trusted companion; for the lady was speaking to her as they passed out through the gate, and there could certainly be no reason for offering any obstruction to any servant of hers.

If there were any fear or excitement in Gertrude's breast as she and her husband passed out of the gate and rode quickly along the path which led through the town, she did not betray it by look or gesture. Her eagerness was mainly showed by a desire to push on northward as fast as possible, and the light of a full harvest moon made travelling almost as easy as by day. On they rode, by sleeping hamlets and dreaming pastures, until the lights of Windsor lay twinkling in the dim, hazy distance miles away.

Evelyn Everett-Green

Then Gertrude suddenly threw back her hood, and leaning towards her companion—they two had outridden their followers some time before—cried in a strange, tense voice:

"O Wendot husband, thou art free! Tomorrow will see us safe within those halls of which thou art rightful lord. Captivity, trouble, peril is at an end. Nothing can greatly hurt us now, for are we not one in bonds that no man may dissever?"

"My noble, true-hearted wife," said Wendot, in accents of intense feeling; and then he leaned forward and kissed her in the whispering wood, and they rode forward through the glades of silvery moonlight towards the new life that was awaiting them beyond.

"Hills, wild rocks, woods, and water!" cried Wendot, with a sudden kindling gleam in his eyes. "O Gertrude, thou didst not tell me the half! I never guessed that England had aught so like home as this. Truly it might be Dynevor itself—that brawling torrent, those craggy fells, and these gray stone walls. And to be free—free to breathe the fresh wind, to go where the fancy prompts, to be loosed from all control save the sweet bonds that thou boldest me in, dearest! Ah, my wife, thou knowest not what thou hast done for me. How shall I thank thee for the boon?"

"Why, by being thine old self again, Vychan," said Gertrude, who was standing by her husband's side on a natural terrace of rock above the Hall which was to be their home. She had brought him out early in the morning to see the sun rise upon their home, and the rapture of his face, the passionate joy she saw written there, was more than she had hoped for.

"Thou hast grown old and worn of late, too saddened, too grave for thy years. Thou must grow young again, and be the bright-faced youth to whom I gave my heart. Thy youth is not left so far behind but what thou canst recall it ere it be too late."

"In sooth I shall grow young again here, sweetheart," quoth Wendot, or Vychan, as we must call him now. He had an equal right to that name with his father, though for convenience he had always been addressed by the other; and now that Lady Gertrude had brought her husband home, he was to be known as Res Vychan, one of the descendants of the last princes of South Wales, who had taken his wife's name also, as he was now the ruler of her land; so, according to the fashion of the English people, he would henceforth be known as Vychan Cherleton. His brother's name he could not bear to hear applied to himself, and it was left to Joanna to explain matters to the king and queen when the chance should arrive. None else need ever know that the husband of the Lady Gertrude had ever been a captive of Edward's; and the name of Griffeth ap Res Vychan disappears from the ken of the chroniclers as if it had never been known that he was once a prisoner in England.

There was no pursuit made after the missing Welshman. The king and queen had other matters to think of, and the fondness of their son for the youth would have been protection enough even if he had not begged with his dying breath that his father would forgive and forget. Lady Gertrude and her husband did not come to court for very many years; and by the time they did so, Vychan Cherleton's loyalty and service to the English cause were too well established for any one to raise a question as to his birth or race.

If the king and queen ever knew they had been outwitted by their children, they did not resent that this had been so, nor that an act of mercy had been contrived greater than they might have felt justified in ratifying.

But all this was yet in the future. As Vychan and his wife stood on that high plateau overlooking the fair valley of the Derwent, it seemed to Gertrude as though during the past three days her husband had undergone some subtle change. There was a new light in his eyes; his frame had lost its drooping air of languor; he had stood the long days of rough riding without the smallest fatigue. It really seemed as if the old Wendot had come back again, and she smilingly asked him how it was that he had gained such strength in so short a time.

"Ah, that question is soon answered, sweet wife. It is freedom that is the elixir of life to us sons of Cambria. I know not if your English-born men can brook the sense of fetter and constraint, but it is death to us.

"Let us not think of it more. That page has closed for ever; and never shall it reopen, for sooner will I die than fall alive into the hands of a foe. Nay, sweetest Gertrude, look not so reproachfully at me. Thou shalt soon see that I mean not to die, but to live for thee. Here in this fair, free spot we begin our new life together. It may be even yet—for see, is not that bright sky, illumined by those quivering shafts of light athwart our path, an omen of good?—that as thou showest me this fair spot with which thou hast endowed me, I may one day show thee again and endow thee with the broad lands of Dynevor."

CHAPTER XIII

THE NEW LORD OF DYNEVOR

"Vychan, Vychan, the hour has come! That false traitor Sir Res has risen in revolt against England's king. Loyal men are called upon to put down the rebellion, and such as do so will be rewarded with the lands reft from the traitor. Vychan, Vychan, lose not a moment; arm and take the men, and fly to Dynevor! Now is the time to strike the blow! And I will to Edward's court, to plead with him for the lands and castle of Dynevor as my husband's guerdon for his services. O Vychan, Vychan, have not I always said that thou shouldest live to call thyself Lord of Dynevor again?"

Gertrude came flying to her husband with these words, looking scarce less young and certainly none less bright and happy than she had done four years back, when she and her husband had first stood within the walls of her ancestral home. A beautiful, sturdy boy hung upon her hand, keeping pace gallantly even with her flying steps, and the joy of motherhood had given something of added lustre to the soft beauty of her dark eyes; otherwise she was scarce changed from the Gertrude of past days. As for Vychan, he still retained the eagle glance, the almost boyish freshness of colouring, and the soldier-like bearing which distinguished his race, and the gold of his hair had not tarnished or faded,

Evelyn Everett-Green

though he had developed from the youth to the man, and was a noble specimen of manhood in the zenith of its strength and beauty.

Rising hastily at his wife's approach, he gazed at her with parted lips and glowing eyes, whilst she once more told him the news, brought by a special messenger from the Princess Joanna, brought thus, as both knew, with a special meaning which they well understood. Four years of peaceful prosperity in England had in no whit weakened Vychan's love for his own land or blunted the soldier-like instincts of his race. There was something of the light of battle and of conquest in his eye as he gazed at his wife, and his voice rang out clear and trumpet-like as he gathered the sense of the message she brought.

"Take up arms against that false traitor-kinsman of mine? ay, verily, that I will. False first to his kindred and his country, then false to the king who has trusted and rewarded him so nobly. Res ap Meredith, methinks thine hour is come! Thou didst plot and contrive to wrest from me the fair lands my father bequeathed me; but I trow the day has dawned when the false lord shall be cast forth, even as he has cast forth others, and when there shall be a lord of the old race ruling at Dynevor, albeit he rule beneath a new name."

"Heaven grant it may be so!" cried Gertrude, the tears of excitement sparkling in her eyes; whilst little Griffeth, catching some of the sense of his father's words, and understanding with the quick instinct of childhood that there was something unwonted going on, shook his little fist in the air, and cried:

"Dynevor, Dynevor! me fight for Dynevor, too."

The father picked up his son and held him in a close embrace.

"Ay, Griffeth, my man, thou shalt reign at Dynevor one of these days, please God to give us victory over false friends and traitorous allies."

And even as the parents stood looking smilingly at the brave child, the blast from the warder's trumpet gave notice that strangers were approaching the Hall; and hurrying to the entrance gate to be ready to receive the guests, Vychan and his wife beheld a little troop of horsemen winding their way up the valley, headed by a pair who appeared to be man and wife, and to hold some exalted position, for the trappings of their steeds and the richness of their own dress marked them as of no humble rank.

Visitors were sufficiently rare at this lonely place for this sight to cause some stir in the Hall; and Gertrude, shading her eyes with her hand, gazed eagerly at the two figures in advance. Suddenly she gave a little cry of rapture, and bounded forward through the gateway.

"It is Arthyn—Arthyn and Llewelyn! Vychan, thy brother and his wife are here. Oh, they have come to bid thee to the fray! They bring tidings, and are come to summon thee to the fight.

"Arthyn, sweetest sister, ten thousand welcomes to our home! Nay, I can scarce believe this is not a dream. How I have longed to see thee here!"

Vychan was at his brother's side, as Arthyn, flinging herself from her saddle, flew into Gertrude's arms. For some moments nothing could be distinguished but the glad clamour of welcome, and scarce had that subsided before it recommenced in the eager salutations of the Welsh retainers, who saw in Vychan another of the sons of their well-loved Lord, Res Vychan, the former Lord of Dynevor and

Iscennen, whose wise and merciful rule had never been forgotten.

Vychan was touched, indeed, to see how well he was remembered, and the sound of the familiar tongue sent thrills of strange emotion through him. It was some time before he could free himself from the throng of servants who pressed round him; and when he could do so he followed his wife and guests into the banqueting hall, where the noonday repast was spread, giving charge to his seneschal for the hospitable entertainment of the retinue his brother had brought and their lodgment within the walls of the Hall.

When he reached the inner hall he found the servants spreading the best viands of the house upon the table; whilst Gertrude, Arthyn, and Llewelyn were gathered together in the embrasure of a window in eager discussion. Gertrude broke away and came quickly towards him, her face deeply flushed and her eyes very bright.

"Vychan, it is even as we have heard. That false traitor is in open revolt, and he has been even more false than we knew. What think you of this?—he professed to be sorry for his revolt, and sent a letter of urgent pleading to Llewelyn and Arthyn begging them to use their influence with the king to obtain his pardon. Believing him to be sincere, Llewelyn set out for England not more than two short weeks back, taking with him, on account of the unsettled state of the country, the pick of the men from Carregcennen. And when this double-dyed traitor knows that Arthyn is alone and unprotected in the castle, what does he do but send a strong band of his soldiers, himself at their head, who obtain entrance by the subterranean passage, slay the guard, and take possession of the fortress. Arthyn has but bare time to escape with a handful of men, and by hard riding to join her husband on the road to England.

"So now have they turned aside to tell the tale to us, and to summon thee to come with thy men and fight in the king's quarrel against this wicked man. And whilst ye lead your soldiers into Wales, Arthyn and I will to the court, to lay the story before the royal Edward, and to gain from him the full and free grants of the castles of Dynevor and Carregcennen for our husbands, who have responded to his call, and have flown to wrest from the traitor the possession he has so unrighteously grasped."

"Thy wife speaketh wise words, Vychan," said Llewelyn, whose dark brows wore a threatening look, and who had the appearance of a man deeply stirred to wrath, as indeed he well might be; "and it were well that we lost no time in dallying here. How many men canst thou summon to thy banner, and when can we be on the march for the south? The Earl of Cornwall has been called upon to quell this revolt, and he has summoned to his aid all loyal subjects of the king who hold dear the peace and prosperity of their land.

"The days are gone by in which I should despise that call and join the standard of revolt. The experience of the past has taught me that in the English alliance is Wales's only hope of tranquillity and true independence and civilization. When such men as this Res ap Meredith break into revolt against Edward, it is time for us to rally round his standard. What would our lives, our lands, our liberties be worth were such a double-distilled traitor as he transformed into a prince, as is his fond ambition?"

"True, Llewelyn, true. The race of kings has vanished from Wales, and methinks there is no humiliation in owning as sovereign lord the lion-hearted King of England. Moreover, has he not given us a prince of our own, born upon Welsh soil, sprung of a kingly race? We will rally round the standard of father and son, and trust that in the future a

Evelyn Everett-Green

brighter day will dawn for our long-distracted country."

So forthwith there sped messengers through the wild valleys and wilder fells of Derbyshire, and many a sturdy son of the mountains came gladly and willingly at the call of the feudal lord whose wise and kindly rule had made him greatly beloved. The fighting instinct of the age and of the race was speedily aroused by this call to arms, and the surrounding gentlemen and yeomen of the county likewise pressed their services upon Vychan, glad to be able to strike a blow to uphold the authority of a king whose wise and brave rule had already made him the idol of the nation.

It was a goodly sight to see the brothers of Dynevor (as their wives could not but call them once again) ride forth at the head of this well-equipped following. Llewelyn marvelled at the discipline displayed by the recruits—a discipline decidedly in advance of anything his own ruder followers could boast. But Welsh and English for once were in brotherly accord, and rode shoulder to shoulder in all good fellowship; and the English knew that their ruder comrades from Cambria, if less well trained and drilled, would be able to show them a lesson in fierce and desperate fighting, to which they were far more inured than their more peaceable neighbours from the sister country.

And fighting there was for all; but the struggle, if fierce, was brief. Sir Res was a coward at heart, as it is the wont of a traitor to be, and finding himself opposed by foes as relentless and energetic as Vychan and Llewelyn, he was speedily driven from fortress to fortress, till at length he was forced to surrender himself a prisoner to the Earl of Gloucester; who, out of kindness to his wife, Auda de Hastings, connived at his escape to Ireland.

There he lived in seclusion for some time; but the spirit of rebellion was still alive within him, and two years later he returned to Wales, and succeeded in collecting an army of four thousand turbulent spirits about him, at the head of which force he fought a pitched battle with the king's justiciary, Robert de Tibetot. His army was cut to pieces. He was taken prisoner himself, and met a cruel death at York as the reward of his many acts of treasonable rebellion.

But the halls of Dynevor saw him no more from the moment when Res Vychan, with a swelling heart, first drove him forth, and planted his own foot once again upon the soil dearer to him than any other spot on earth. As he stood upon the familiar terrace, looking over the wide, fair valley of the Towy, his heart swelled with thankfulness and joy; and if a slow, unwonted tear found its way to his eye, it was scarce a tear of sorrow, for he felt assured that his brother Griffeth was sharing in the joy of this restoration to the old home, and that his loving and gentle spirit was not very far from him at this supreme hour of his life.

"Father, father, father!"

Vychan turned with a start at the sound of the joyous call, and the next moment was clasping wife and son to his breast.

"Sweetheart! come so quickly? How couldst thou?"

"Ay, Vychan, love hath ever wings, and neither I nor Arthyn could keep away, our business at the court once accomplished. Vychan, husband, thou standest here Lord of Dynevor in thine own right. Thou hast won back thine ancestral home, the boy's inheritance.

"Seest thou this deed? Knowest thou the king's seal? Take it, for it secureth all to thee under thy name of Vychan Cherleton. And if in times to come those who come after know not that it

Evelyn Everett-Green

was the son of Res Vychan who thus reclaimed his patrimony, and if our worthy chroniclers set down that Dynevor and its lands passed to the keeping of the English, what matters it? We know the truth, and those who have loved thee and thy father know who thou art and whence thou hast come. Let that be sufficient for thee and for me.

"Griffeth, little son, kiss thy father, and bid him welcome to his own halls again—the halls of Dynevor."

Vychan could not speak. He pressed one passionate kiss upon the lips of his wife, and another upon the brow of his noble boy, who looked every inch a Dynevor, with the true Dynevor features, and the bold, fearless mien so like his father's.

Then commanding himself by an effort, he opened the king's parchment and quickly mastered its contents, after which he took his wife's hand and held out the other to his son.

"My faithful fellows are mustering in the hall to bid me welcome once more to Dynevor. Come, sweet wife; I must show to them their lady and their future lord.

"Arthyn—where is she? Has she gone on to Iscennen to meet Llewelyn there?"

"Ay, verily: she was as hungry for him as I for thee; and she hath a similar mandate for him regarding his rights to Carregcennen.

"O Vychan, dearest husband, I can scarce believe it is not all a dream."

Indeed, to Vychan it seemed almost as though he dreamed, as in the old familiar hall he stood, a little raised from the crowd of armed retainers upon the steps of the wide oak staircase, as he addressed to them a speech eloquent with that thrilling eloquence which is the gift of all who speak from the heart, and speak to hearts beating in deep and true response. Vychan thanked all those who had so bravely fought for him, explained to all assembled there his new position and his new name, bid them not think him less a Welshman and a Dynevor because he bore his wife's arms and called himself the servant of the English king, and held up before their eyes the mandate of that English king confirming to him the lands and halls of Dynevor.

A wild, ringing cheer broke from all who heard him as he thus proved to their own satisfaction that the royal Edward was their best friend, and as the new Lord of Dynevor held up his child for them to see, and to own as future lord in the time-honoured fashion, such a shout went up from the throats of all as made the vaulted roof ring again. Blades were unsheathed and waved in wild enthusiasm, and Gertrude's dark eyes glistened through a mist of proud and happy tears.

Suddenly from some dim recess in the old ball there issued a strain of wild music—the sound of a harp played by no unskilled hand; whilst mingling with the twang of the strings was the voice of the ancient bard, cracked through age, yet still retaining the old power and some of the old sweetness. And harp and voice were raised alike in one of those triumph songs that have ever been as the elixir of life to the strong, rude, sensitive sons of wild Cambria.

"It is Wenwynwyn," quoth Vychan. "He is yet alive. I little thought to see him more.

"Griffeth, boy, run to yon old man and bid him give thee his blessing, and tell him that there is a son of Dynevor come back to rule as Lord of Dynevor once again."

POSTSCRIPT

The story of the sons of Res Vychan is very intricate and difficult to follow, owing to the lack of contemporaneous documents; but the main facts of their story as related in the foregoing pages are true, though a certain license has been taken for purposes of fiction.

They have been represented as somewhat younger than they were at the time of these events, whilst the children of Edward the First have been made some few years older than their true ages.

There is no actual historical warrant for the change of identity between Wendot and Griffeth, and for the escape and reinstatement of the former in the halls of Dynevor; but there are traditions which point to a possibility that he did escape from prison, in spite of the affirmation of the chroniclers, as there have been those who claim descent from him, which they would hardly have done if such had not been the case, for there is no record that he was married before he was taken prisoner to England.

The children of the English king were not really at Rhuddlan Castle in 1277, as represented here, as they were at that time too young to accompany their father on his expeditions. If, however, they had been as old as represented in these pages, there is little doubt they would have accompanied him, as the monarch was a most affectionate father, and loved to have wife and children about him.

Arthyn is a fictitious character; as is also Gertrude. There is no record that any of the sons of Res Vychan married or left descendants, except the tradition alluded to above.

Evelyn Everett-Green

Choose from Thousands of 1stWorldLibrary Classics By

A. M. Barnard
Ada Leverson
Adolphus William Ward
Aesop
Agatha Christie
Alexander Aaronsohn
Alexander Kielland
Alexandre Dumas
Alfred Gatty
Alfred Ollivant
Alice Duer Miller
Alice Turner Curtis
Alice Dunbar
Allen Chapman
Alleyne Ireland
Ambrose Bierce
Amelia E. Barr
Amory H. Bradford
Andrew Lang
Andrew McFarland Davis
Andy Adams
Angela Brazil
Anna Alice Chapin
Anna Sewell
Annie Besant
Annie Hamilton Donnell
Annie Payson Call
Annie Roe Carr
Annonaymous
Anton Chekhov
Archibald Lee Fletcher
Arnold Bennett
Arthur C. Benson
Arthur Conan Doyle
Arthur M. Winfield
Arthur Ransome
Arthur Schnitzler
Arthur Train
Atticus
B.H. Baden-Powell
B. M. Bower
B. C. Chatterjee
Baroness Emmuska Orczy
Baroness Orczy
Basil King
Bayard Taylor
Ben Macomber
Bertha Muzzy Bower
Bjornstjerne Bjornson

Booth Tarkington
Boyd Cable
Bram Stoker
C. Collodi
C. E. Orr
C. M. Ingleby
Carolyn Wells
Catherine Parr Traill
Charles A. Eastman
Charles Amory Beach
Charles Dickens
Charles Dudley Warner
Charles Farrar Browne
Charles Ives
Charles Kingsley
Charles Klein
Charles Hanson Towne
Charles Lathrop Pack
Charles Romyn Dake
Charles Whibley
Charles Willing Beale
Charlotte M. Braeme
Charlotte M. Yonge
Charlotte Perkins Stetson
Clair W. Hayes
Clarence Day Jr.
Clarence E. Mulford
Clemence Housman
Confucius
Coningsby Dawson
Cornelis DeWitt Wilcox
Cyril Burleigh
D. H. Lawrence
Daniel Defoe
David Garnett
Dinah Craik
Don Carlos Janes
Donald Keyhoe
Dorothy Kilner
Dougan Clark
Douglas Fairbanks
E. Nesbit
E. P. Roe
E. Phillips Oppenheim
E. S. Brooks
Earl Barnes
Edgar Rice Burroughs
Edith Van Dyne
Edith Wharton

Edward Everett Hale
Edward J. O'Biren
Edward S. Ellis
Edwin L. Arnold
Eleanor Atkins
Eleanor Hallowell Abbott
Eliot Gregory
Elizabeth Gaskell
Elizabeth McCracken
Elizabeth Von Arnim
Ellem Key
Emerson Hough
Emilie F. Carlen
Emily Bronte
Emily Dickinson
Enid Bagnold
Enilor Macartney Lane
Erasmus W. Jones
Ernie Howard Pie
Ethel May Dell
Ethel Turner
Ethel Watts Mumford
Eugene Sue
Eugenie Foa
Eugene Wood
Eustace Hale Ball
Evelyn Everett-green
Everard Cotes
F. H. Cheley
F. J. Cross
F. Marion Crawford
Fannie E. Newberry
Federick Austin Ogg
Ferdinand Ossendowski
Fergus Hume
Florence A. Kilpatrick
Fremont B. Deering
Francis Bacon
Francis Darwin
Frances Hodgson Burnett
Frances Parkinson Keyes
Frank Gee Patchin
Frank Harris
Frank Jewett Mather
Frank L. Packard
Frank V. Webster
Frederic Stewart Isham
Frederick Trevor Hill
Frederick Winslow Taylor

Friedrich Kerst
Friedrich Nietzsche
Fyodor Dostoyevsky
G.A. Henty
G.K. Chesterton
Gabrielle E. Jackson
Garrett P. Serviss
Gaston Leroux
George A. Warren
George Ade
Geroge Bernard Shaw
George Cary Eggleston
George Durston
George Ebers
George Eliot
George Gissing
George MacDonald
George Meredith
George Orwell
George Sylvester Viereck
George Tucker
George W. Cable
George Wharton James
Gertrude Atherton
Gordon Casserly
Grace E. King
Grace Gallatin
Grace Greenwood
Grant Allen
Guillermo A. Sherwell
Gulielma Zollinger
Gustav Flaubert
H. A. Cody
H. B. Irving
H.C. Bailey
H. G. Wells
H. H. Munro
H. Irving Hancock
H. R. Naylor
H. Rider Haggard
H. W. C. Davis
Haldeman Julius
Hall Caine
Hamilton Wright Mabie
Hans Christian Andersen
Harold Avery
Harold McGrath
Harriet Beecher Stowe
Harry Castlemon
Harry Coghill
Harry Houidini

Hayden Carruth
Helent Hunt Jackson
Helen Nicolay
Hendrik Conscience
Hendy David Thoreau
Henri Barbusse
Henrik Ibsen
Henry Adams
Henry Ford
Henry Frost
Henry James
Henry Jones Ford
Henry Seton Merriman
Henry W Longfellow
Herbert A. Giles
Herbert Carter
Herbert N. Casson
Herman Hesse
Hildegard G. Frey
Homer
Honore De Balzac
Horace B. Day
Horace Walpole
Horatio Alger Jr.
Howard Pyle
Howard R. Garis
Hugh Lofting
Hugh Walpole
Humphry Ward
Ian Maclaren
Inez Haynes Gillmore
Irving Bacheller
Isabel Cecilia Williams
Isabel Hornibrook
Israel Abrahams
Ivan Turgenev
J.G.Austin
J. Henri Fabre
J. M. Barrie
J. M. Walsh
J. Macdonald Oxley
J. R. Miller
J. S. Fletcher
J. S. Knowles
J. Storer Clouston
J. W. Duffield
Jack London
Jacob Abbott
James Allen
James Andrews
James Baldwin

James Branch Cabell
James DeMille
James Joyce
James Lane Allen
James Lane Allen
James Oliver Curwood
James Oppenheim
James Otis
James R. Driscoll
Jane Abbott
Jane Austen
Jane L. Stewart
Janet Aldridge
Jens Peter Jacobsen
Jerome K. Jerome
Jessie Graham Flower
John Buchan
John Burroughs
John Cournos
John F. Kennedy
John Gay
John Glasworthy
John Habberton
John Joy Bell
John Kendrick Bangs
John Milton
John Philip Sousa
John Taintor Foote
Jonas Lauritz Idemil Lie
Jonathan Swift
Joseph A. Altsheler
Joseph Carey
Joseph Conrad
Joseph E. Badger Jr
Joseph Hergesheimer
Joseph Jacobs
Jules Vernes
Julian Hawthrone
Julie A Lippmann
Justin Huntly McCarthy
Kakuzo Okakura
Karle Wilson Baker
Kate Chopin
Kenneth Grahame
Kenneth McGaffey
Kate Langley Bosher
Kate Langley Bosher
Katherine Cecil Thurston
Katherine Stokes
L. A. Abbot
L. T. Meade

L. Frank Baum
Latta Griswold
Laura Dent Crane
Laura Lee Hope
Laurence Housman
Lawrence Beasley
Leo Tolstoy
Leonid Andreyev
Lewis Carroll
Lewis Sperry Chafer
Lilian Bell
Lloyd Osbourne
Louis Hughes
Louis Joseph Vance
Louis Tracy
Louisa May Alcott
Lucy Fitch Perkins
Lucy Maud Montgomery
Luther Benson
Lydia Miller Middleton
Lyndon Orr
M. Corvus
M. H. Adams
Margaret E. Sangster
Margret Howth
Margaret Vandercook
Margaret W. Hungerford
Margret Penrose
Maria Edgeworth
Maria Thompson Daviess
Mariano Azuela
Marion Polk Angellotti
Mark Overton
Mark Twain
Mary Austin
Mary Catherine Crowley
Mary Cole
Mary Hastings Bradley
Mary Roberts Rinehart
Mary Rowlandson
M. Wollstonecraft Shelley
Maud Lindsay
Max Beerbohm
Myra Kelly
Nathaniel Hawthrone
Nicolo Machiavelli
O. F. Walton
Oscar Wilde

Owen Johnson
P.G. Wodehouse
Paul and Mabel Thorne
Paul G. Tomlinson
Paul Severing
Percy Brebner
Percy Keese Fitzhugh
Peter B. Kyne
Plato
Quincy Allen
R. Derby Holmes
R. L. Stevenson
R. S. Ball
Rabindranath Tagore
Rahul Alvares
Ralph Bonehill
Ralph Henry Barbour
Ralph Victor
Ralph Waldo Emmerson
Rene Descartes
Ray Cummings
Rex Beach
Rex E. Beach
Richard Harding Davis
Richard Jefferies
Richard Le Gallienne
Robert Barr
Robert Frost
Robert Gordon Anderson
Robert L. Drake
Robert Lansing
Robert Lynd
Robert Michael Ballantyne
Robert W. Chambers
Rosa Nouchette Carey
Rudyard Kipling
Saint Augustine
Samuel B. Allison
Samuel Hopkins Adams
Sarah Bernhardt
Sarah C. Hallowell
Selma Lagerlof
Sherwood Anderson
Sigmund Freud
Standish O'Grady
Stanley Weyman
Stella Benson
Stella M. Francis

Stephen Crane
Stewart Edward White
Stijn Streuvels
Swami Abhedananda
Swami Parmananda
T. S. Ackland
T. S. Arthur
The Princess Der Ling
Thomas A. Janvier
Thomas A Kempis
Thomas Anderton
Thomas Bailey Aldrich
Thomas Bulfinch
Thomas De Quincey
Thomas Dixon
Thomas H. Huxley
Thomas Hardy
Thomas More
Thornton W. Burgess
U. S. Grant
Upton Sinclair
Valentine Williams
Various Authors
Vaughan Kester
Victor Appleton
Victor G. Durham
Victoria Cross
Virginia Woolf
Wadsworth Camp
Walter Camp
Walter Scott
Washington Irving
Wilbur Lawton
Wilkie Collins
Willa Cather
Willard F. Baker
William Dean Howells
William le Queux
W. Makepeace Thackeray
William W. Walter
William Shakespeare
Winston Churchill
Yei Theodora Ozaki
Yogi Ramacharaka
Young E. Allison
Zane Grey